Best Wishes!

"Chosen to Live"

THE INSPIRING STORY OF FLIGHT 232 SURVIVOR JERRY SCHEMMEL

Jerry Schemmel
with Kevin Simpson

"Chosen to Live"
by Jerry Schemmel
with Kevin Simpson

Victory Publishing Company
P. O. Box 621129
Littleton, CO 80162

Book Design by Robert Howard Graphic Design

ISBN 0-9652086-5-6
Library of Congress Catalog Card Number: 96-090387

10 9 8 7 6 5 4 3 2

For the 112 who didn't make it.

Contents

Chapter

1

I WAS NEVER
"FEARLESS"

It's an early afternoon in the autumn of 1993 and I'm sitting in the dark in Sacramento, watching a sliver of my life played out on a movie theater's giant screen. I suppose that in some private moment we all have imagined our stories told larger than life, but this isn't exactly what I had in mind.

In the very first scene, I see myself portrayed by actor Jeff Bridges — so far, so good — walking through a haze of smoke and out of a cornfield. I am carrying a baby from the remains of a burning airplane whose fuselage has been shredded across a stretch of Midwestern farmland. I am a survivor. I am a hero. And I have become, as the movie hints in its title and goes on to illustrate with its account of the disquieting aftermath of the crash, <u>Fearless</u>.

Reality check: I am no Jeff Bridges — although my wife, Diane, in a surge of marital diplomacy, once suggested that the lead role in my life story ought to be played by Kevin Costner. I am no Max Klein, the screen name for the character played by Bridges. I am still just Jerry Schemmel, and the afternoon movie is simply a break in my job describing the heroics of others — specifically, professional basketball players. I am a television and radio play-by-play announcer for the National Basketball Association's Denver Nuggets.

Although a chain of improbable events did, in fact, once lead me to carry a baby from the wreckage of a burning airplane, the act was reflexively human and not heroic. But the opening scene of the movie reminded me, for the millionth time, of two irrefutable facts. First, it was my misfortune to be the last passenger to step onto United Airlines Flight 232 when it left Denver, bound for Chicago, on July 19, 1989. Second, it was my inexplicable good fortune to remain alive after the DC-10, crippled in mid-flight, crashed at Sioux Gateway Airport in Sioux City, Iowa, during an emergency landing.

Videotape of this fiery climax played over every television station in America in the weeks, months and years afterward, becoming the most watched piece of news footage in American television history. Every time I watched, it reminded me that I should be dead. Miraculously, 184 of the 296 passengers and crew aboard the plane survived.

Many of us became friends, bonded by common psychological scars and this disquieting mixture of tragedy and luck, but we did not experience the overwhelming feelings of fearlessness this film suggested. No one in my circle of acquaintances from the crash felt the rush of invincibility that became the cornerstone for the fictional book and film, both titled <u>Fearless</u>, that mirrored so many details from the actual events of United 232. To the contrary, we felt our mortality squeezed to the surface until we wore it like a second skin.

Still, <u>Fearless</u> became a crucial experience for me, even though it wasn't released until four years after United 232 went down. By the memories it stirred and the anger it ignited, the movie became a litmus test for my psychological and spiritual recovery, or what I'd come to perceive as my emergence from guilt and self-pity en route to some semblance of normalcy. One thing a devastating experience like surviving a plane crash teaches is to never completely trust immediate reactions, emotions and decisions. In the months and years following the incident, many survivors veered off on strange and frightening emotional tangents. Those journeys did not become apparent to us until much later, when with the benefit of hindsight we could look back and see the vapor trails left by these difficult times in our lives.

Recovery has been a long and continuous process, a succession of incremental gains and sudden setbacks. And it is surely not over. We can come to grips with the fear, intense introspection and regret we felt during the 45-minute gap between the time the rear engine exploded, severing the hydraulic system that steered the plane, and the moment we started our fiery slide along the runway in Sioux City. But — and here I must speak strictly for myself — not one day passes that I don't consider the experience, if only for a moment in the morning while looking into the bathroom mirror, and feel its reverberations. Guilt and anger recede into depression and self-pity, only to emerge as a different kind of anger that becomes transformed, many times, into determination. For me and many others who survived United 232, backslides into depression have ended with the soul emerging somehow intact, even energized. The process is sometimes deceptively subtle, but always relentless, never-ending.

Surviving United 232 made us feel different, but not necessarily diminished. There is the feeling of being scarred for life, but there is also the feeling of being baptized into a sort of communion of unlikely survivors, survivors whose reason for living takes the shape of day-to-day revelations that can seem alarming in their complexity, or disarming in their simplicity.

The November afternoon in Sacramento, where the Nuggets were preparing to play the Kings, didn't seem like the time or place for any sort of cosmic revelation. There was simply a game-day afternoon to be occupied, one of those dead spots in the schedule that fans don't consider when they contemplate the glamor of professional sports. Players typically rest in their rooms, recovering from the physical pounding inflicted by an 82-game regular-season schedule and the occasional well-placed elbow, and order room service or perhaps wander to the hotel restaurant. On some trips, the NBA media contingent simply fights boredom. Writers from the daily newspapers might work on some advance stories, the television people might have technical details to attend to and a radio play-by-play man can update his information on that night's opponent, but the work never seems to sufficiently expand to fill the time on the road. A movie can consume a sizable chunk of the day and, linked with prolonged restaurant visits and a couple of passes through a shopping mall, take us comfortably to tip-off.

Film selection is never a very scientific process, as the opportunities to kill time in theaters over a season that lasts eight months — longer if the team progresses through the playoffs — far outnumber the offerings. Around the time the team headed to Sacramento, it just so happened that I'd read some newspaper articles about the release of <u>Fearless</u>. It was in one of these stories that I first learned that the plot was, in part, based on some elements of the crash of United 232. Beyond that, I knew only that there was a rather remarkable recreation of a crash scene and that Jeff Bridges played the male lead.

The meaning behind the title still mystified me and added to my curiosity, which at that moment outweighed any discomfort about watching the film. Besides, I considered myself basically recovered from the trauma of my experience, or at least recovered as far as seemed humanly possible. That is to say, I was handling it and moving ahead with my life. I was starting my second season doing radio play-by-play for the Nuggets, a job that allowed me to virtually live out a professional dream. Only three months earlier, I'd seen a trauma counselor and gotten what sounded to me like a clean bill of mental health. I wasn't so naive as to believe that all traces of the ordeal had been washed from my life, but I felt confident in my ability to deal with this part of my past. The movie, it seemed, was nothing I couldn't handle.

Scott Hastings had finished his playing career the year before, with the Nuggets, and now was learning the ropes as a broadcaster doing color commentary for the team's televised games. He was never mistaken for an NBA star, but his mind for the game, his toughness and the leadership qualities he learned during a championship season with the Detroit Pistons had made him valuable to a young Denver team as a player in a backup role. He was sort of a tutor — less physically gifted than the men who played most of the minutes, but invaluable for his wisdom and locker room demeanor. His insights to the game and his wonderful and somewhat famous sense of humor gave him all the raw material he would need to succeed as a broadcaster. We'd become good friends during his final season in uniform and now that he'd joined the media contingent, we found ourselves keeping company pretty frequently on the road. He was a perfect movie companion.

As we walked the few blocks from our hotel to the theater multiplex in Sacramento, I admitted some apprehension about seeing Fearless. The feeling surprised me, but didn't seem daunting enough to make me turn back. Then came the opening scene, the too-familiar scene of smoke swirling through a cornfield and a man carrying a baby in his arms. The recognition was, of course, instantaneous for me. The overwhelming sensation was one of wonder and curiosity. Someone had gotten inside my head, had gained access to my personal memory archives, and made a movie about part of my life. That's how precise the detail seemed in that first shot. Only seconds into the movie, I was wondering if Jeff Bridges would go on to become an NBA broadcaster. Hastings, one of those people who likes to add his own humorous narration to films, leaned over and offered an uncommonly serious observation.

"This looks like you, Schemmel," he said.

I thought there would be more conversation. Hastings usually produced an almost parallel soundtrack to a movie, chiming in with commentary and one-liners. It made no difference if the film was a comedy, an action thriller or serious art. He found a way to wring the humor out of it. Yet during <u>Fearless</u>, he fell quiet after that first exchange. It was so unusual that I became quite conscious of his silence and wondered if the film's intensity had affected him. Later, I learned that he didn't speak simply out of respect for me. Naturally, Scott couldn't know how close some aspects of the movie brushed against my own reality, but he suspected that fiction might be venturing too close for comfort for me. He was correct.

As the film moved on, other striking details of my experience appeared before my eyes. Bridges' partner and best friend dies in the crash. So did mine. A woman sitting near Bridges has a two-year-old boy who also dies. That, too, mirrored my experience. Bridges plays an architect. At the time, I was also a professional, working as deputy commissioner and legal counsel for the Continental Basketball Association, sort of a minor league to the NBA. Bridges tries to comfort a youngster during the traumatic time between the mid-air explosion and the horrible touchdown. So did I. Bridges rescues an infant from the wreckage. I did the same thing.

Eventually, though, the plot of the movie took twists and turns that had absolutely nothing to do with Jerry Schemmel and, in fact, ran counter to the overriding theme of my experience. Nevertheless, while watching the film, I found one very troubling question about the making of <u>Fearless</u> forcing its way into my mind: Why hadn't I heard about this film before it was released?

It was perhaps one-third of the way through the movie that, in spite of my certainty that I had recovered from the worst effects of the crash, I began to feel just a little exploited. That might seem a strange feeling, coming from a sports media type who draws some measure of notoriety from the reflected glare of athletes in the public eye. Maybe as someone who works in the sports sector of the entertainment industry, I should have shrugged, or at least absorbed the initial shock and written it all off as the price one pays for being in the public eye. After all, I had been no stranger to the spotlight in the immediate aftermath of United 232's well-chronicled crash. Pieces of my story were told repeatedly in newspapers and on television stations around the world, until it almost seemed that this terrifying chunk of my life had become public domain. I did not wince then — in fact, my wife compiled three scrapbooks of clippings — but watching selected details, painful details, materialize in a darkened theater caught me off-guard.

Adding to my growing discomfort was the fact that while certain aspects of the Jeff Bridges character were unquestionably based on me, much more of his reaction to the crash conflicted sharply with my own.

His brush with death made him fearless, inspired feelings of invincibility at having survived so devastating an experience. My own overriding feeling was the opposite. It was one of vulnerability. He became cold and distant. I may have become slightly detached, but I still sought solace among friends and family. He tested fate with suicidal acts, like walking the ledge of a skyscraper and running across eight lanes of busy interstate highway. I did nothing of the kind, although probably half a dozen people, including good friends and even a couple family members who eventually watched the movie, later awkwardly remarked that they'd had no idea I'd attempted suicide. A few also wondered, prompted by Bridges' on-screen relationship with co-star Rosie Perez, if I'd had an affair with another crash survivor. Of course, nothing could be further from the truth. So sitting there in Sacramento, watching the film take what seemed like more and more outrageous liberties with my life, I felt anger and resentment smoldering. If they were going to do it, why couldn't they do it right? Why couldn't they have portrayed me the way I was, the way I am? And again the gnawing question: Why hadn't I heard about this?

Admittedly, this was no way to judge a film's artistic merit, using my own life as a yardstick to measure the worth of what was claimed to be, despite its allusions to United 232, a piece of fictitious drama. But the movie's departures from my own experience came sandwiched between two scenes of such remarkable and wrenching familiarity that the idea of objectivity on my part was out of the question.

If the opening scene in the cornfield grabbed my attention, then the final flashback scene of the actual crash sent my mind once again careening down the runway in Sioux City. That finale might have lasted a minute or two, but it totally absorbed me with sight lines and camera angles that seemed like cinema of the mind — my mind. I could feel myself shaking and, against all logic, wondered for a few seconds if I really was in a Sacramento movie theater or an Iowa cornfield.

As the closing credits rolled, Scott Hastings got up to leave. I sat there, still trembling, momentarily separated by the sheer force of cinematography from my earlier feelings of anger and betrayal. A moment later, after gaining some composure, I stood up and walked out.

We didn't say much on the walk back to the hotel. When we arrived, I went to my room and just sat there thinking for a good half-hour or longer, sifting through my anger and trying to get a better grip on it. The phone rang, but I couldn't bring myself to answer it.

There was a momentary reflex that urged me to call Diane, to relate the bizarre and disturbing experience at the theater, but I resisted it. She would be sitting a thousand miles away at our home in Denver, listening to her husband, the man who thought he'd managed to move on with his life, ramble on like some shell-shocked soldier living a flashback. I knew there would be nothing she could do but worry. There was also a part of me that didn't want her to know about this setback. So I stewed by myself, feeling exploited, even violated as I wondered how other people would perceive the movie — particularly people who knew me, or at least thought they did until they saw Jeff Bridges make two passes at taking his own life and become emotionally involved with a fellow survivor. Fortunately, the day's schedule didn't leave me too much time for contemplation. Less than two hours after returning from the movie, the team and the media contingent caught the 5:45 p.m. bus for Arco Arena.

There's a dynamic on a team bus much like there is in any sports locker room, where people drawn together to do a job over a long, arduous season can expose open wounds in their personal lives to an audience that, for all the merciless ribbing it might dish out, nonetheless provides an atmosphere of comfort and support. Some of it is just the superficial chit-chat of the job, and some of it is sincere. All I know is that when I stepped on the bus, I felt comfortable relating the experience in the movie theater and felt emotionally reinforced by the reaction of my colleagues.

Dan Issel, the Hall of Fame center who'd become the Nuggets' head coach and a good friend, became visibly angry that the film had borrowed bits of my experience — significant bits — without bothering to ask. Seeing his reaction, his displeasure at the idea of Hollywood playing havoc with the real lives of the crash victims, made me feel that my initial anger might not have been so far off base. Of course, less than an hour later, when I sat down with him in the arena to tape "The Dan Issel Show," a brief interview that aired on the Nuggets' radio network before every game, he was his old, familiar self. He remarked to Hastings, within earshot, that it was hard for him to believe they got somebody as good-looking as Jeff Bridges to play my part.

9

The movie was on my mind right up until game time, and I recall having to bear down to maintain concentration. Once the flow of the game took over, my professional reflexes returned to normal and so, in the ensuing days, did my attitude about <u>Fearless</u> and the people who made it. The anger subsided and was replaced by a calmer, more rational reaction: It was just a movie, a piece of fiction whose makers drew heavily from the headlines and took all the artistic license they needed to make it a commercial success. Again, the idea that I'm just lucky to still be here, to be alive and even go to the movies in the first place, had a calming influence. It didn't matter if Warner Bros. made a billion dollars from <u>Fearless</u>, because the important thing was my survival, this priceless gift delivered to me for reasons I did not know; this inexplicable reprieve from death that blessed me with second chances I felt I'd done nothing to deserve.

As it turned out, <u>Fearless</u> produced the 14th largest gross revenues of Hollywood's 1993 releases. This came to my attention a few weeks later, as I researched the possibility of suing the studio for damages.

The change of heart was hard to explain, except that it came rooted in resurgent anger over working so hard to move ahead with life and then seeing a movie studio exploit such an excruciating experience. Ultimately, the logic of this conclusion broke down. In the aftermath of the crash, as the media descended on Sioux City and sought interviews with survivors, I told my tale repeatedly, yet felt no pangs of exploitation and violation. The film just seemed different, or perhaps caught me at a strange moment when what I thought to be my emotional and psychological recovery suddenly was revealed as something thin and vulnerable.

There had been some press coverage about my reaction to the movie. <u>Sports Illustrated</u> did a short article in its "Scorecard" segment after being alerted to the episode by the Nuggets beat writer for the <u>Denver Post</u>, Mike Monroe, and a local television station also did a story. Some people prodded me to stand up for myself, not to mention for the rest of the survivors and relatives of the victims, and take action. Because I was trained as a lawyer, and because this is America, it was naturally suggested that I sue. The urgings were enough to move me to research whether I even had a case. Entertainment law certainly isn't my area of expertise, but it appeared at first blush that there were no previous rulings to support any cause of action I might try to bring.

At one point, I actually turned on my home computer and typed out a letter to some executive from Warner Bros. whose name I pulled out of a newspaper article. It wasn't an angry letter, but it stated in no uncertain terms that it would have been nice to know what was coming in <u>Fearless</u>, and that being blindsided by the vivid similarities to the actual story of United 232's crash caused considerable pain and dredged up a lot of bad memories. I never sent it.

Eventually, after talking to so many people — friends, the families of victims, other survivors — I felt a need to try to minimize the damage. It wasn't about money, about real or punitive financial damages. I wanted the studio to give all of us connected to United 232 an apology. I wanted Warner Bros. to admit to us that it shouldn't have done this without at least contacting us first. Personally, I figured a call from a secretary would have been sufficient, anything to give a respectful warning of how closely fiction would mirror portions of our reality. I thought a lot about litigation. Maybe a lawsuit would get somebody's attention.

I decided to dig a little deeper. In the spring of 1994, through some lawyer contacts of mine in Los Angeles, I got hooked up with an attorney, Peter McDonald, an expert in entertainment law. I liked him immediately. After our first telephone conversation, I could tell that he truly cared. First and foremost, he wanted to be sure I understood what I was getting into, that the movie industry did not take lawsuits lightly. He thought that with my media background I'd make a very good and credible witness, but he also made a list of drawbacks to filing suit. Wouldn't it be better to just get on with your life? he asked. What if Warner

11

Bros. dragged out the proceedings and tried to wear you down and run you out of money? Would you still have the stomach for a fight in a year? Two years? But having posed those questions for me to mull, he also said he knew of case law that would definitely weigh in our favor. By the time we talked on the phone again three weeks later, McDonald had seen <u>Fearless</u> three times and researched the court decisions. He figured that if anybody from the actual crash had a case, it was me.

He felt our position was good, but he also felt it would be best to file suit in Colorado rather than California. I concurred. We would be more likely to get a sympathetic jury in my home state than we would in California, where the movie industry wields great power. We spoke once more, when he called to talk about a concern over the statute of limitations. But ultimately we concluded that we were on firm ground and everything was in order if I wanted to proceed with litigation.

Not long after that I sat down and wrote Peter a letter saying that I didn't want to pursue a lawsuit and to send me a bill for his services. He replied in a note that he understood and would charge me nothing. Peter McDonald had been a kind and helpful man. It surprised and saddened me to learn that he died a few months later, at 53, of a heart attack.

The moment I decided to forget about legal action against the movie studio, I knew it was the right choice. It had nothing to do with the legal merits of the case. Maybe we would've won, maybe not, but had we actually gone to jury trial, I liked our chances very much. Although I watched the movie once more and managed to detach myself enough to appreciate it as an entertaining work, my raw reaction to <u>Fearless</u> remained the same. They took my story and exploited it. They caused me a great deal of pain. They made a movie about me and didn't even bother to tell me they were doing it. I will never think that was right; I just don't think it matters. What matters is how I move on, how all of us who survived United 232 or any other life-changing brush with mortality reconstruct ourselves, piece by piece, with the knowledge that we have been spared for a reason.

For me, it always comes back to one simple point: *I could so easily have died in that crash.* That is the element in my life that burdens me with responsibility and, at the same time, offers me opportunity.

Eventually, the movie came to represent a test of sorts, a passage on the way to somewhere better and more solid. It provided a target for anger and indignation, a reservoir for self-pity and a diversion from the difficult business of fitting calamity into context. It was a tool that could chisel the shape of the future into something even more meaningful, yet by seeking some measure of revenge through the legal system, I was in fact drawing dangerously close to bringing down the hammer squarely on my own thumb.

The crash of United 232 still shapes all of the people who survived it. After an experience that was at once tragic and miraculous, moving on with life has required one monumental feat: Reconciliation. Reconciliation of the tragedy. And the miracle.

Chapter

2

THE LAST
PASSENGER

My eyes opened a few minutes before the alarm blared, the way they usually do when I know I have to catch an early-morning flight. I slid out of bed, careful not to disturb my sleeping wife. It was 5:45 by the bedroom clock.

Diane had agreed to drive me to Stapleton International Airport to catch my 7 a.m. flight to Chicago, where I'd make a connection to Columbus, Ohio. In return, I'd promised not to awaken her until the last possible moment before we needed to leave for the five minute ride from our Denver townhouse to the airport. Diane didn't have to be at her job as a membership coordinator for a health-care provider until nine o'clock, and she planned to roll out of bed, drive me to catch my plane and then return with plenty of time to get ready for work.

I stumbled to the bathroom as quietly as I could and went about the unhurried ritual of preparing for a business trip — unhurried because I'd packed my bags the night before. Then I put on a suit and tie. These were not my favorite traveling clothes, but they were necessary because I planned to step off the plane in Columbus and go directly to a meeting.

At the time, I worked as deputy commissioner and legal counsel for the Continental Basketball Association, which is the minor league system of the NBA. We were about to stage our annual draft of player talent, and most of the league officials had already arrived in Columbus. Just two of us from the league office in Denver, myself and commissioner Jay Ramsdell, had decided to tie up loose ends and fly in at the last moment. I'd spent the day before catching up on correspondence, working on a revised standard player contract for the league and touching up part of a presentation we'd soon be making to the NBA, with whom the CBA had a working agreement to train officials and showcase players in return for financial support of a league whose teams play primarily in smaller markets.

It was 6:05 a.m. when I sat down with some coffee and scanned the morning papers. Fifteen minutes later, I went back upstairs and woke Diane. By 6:30, we were on the way to the airport. I drove while Diane more or less eased into consciousness. There wasn't much time or inclination to talk. We had parted this way many times before and had never seemed to pay much attention to the risks of air travel. And it certainly never occurred to us, when she would drop me off at an airport, that we might be mumbling groggy good-byes for the last time.

"I'll call you when I get to Columbus," I said as I pulled my luggage from the trunk and closed the door. We stood for a moment on the sidewalk drop-off area just outside the United Airlines portion of the terminal and hugged. "I love you," I said.

"I love you too, honey," Diane replied.

We each turned and did not look back. Diane drove away, no doubt shifting focus to her day ahead, and I walked off in search of an outdoor television monitor to check my departure gate. I skimmed the list in search of Flight 1614, Denver to Chicago. I found it. Unfortunately, the flight number was followed by a terse announcement: "Canceled."

I turned to see if I could catch Diane before she pulled away and tell her that there would be a change in plans, but it was too late. I decided to call her later, once my travel schedule had been revised. Initially, at least, it didn't seem that the plans would require any major overhaul, as both Denver and Chicago are United hubs and the airline schedules fairly frequent flights between the two cities. Checking another monitor I noted three more morning departures to Chicago: 9:29, 9:30 and 10:30. Odds seemed good that Jay and I could get seats on one of those flights and, with any luck, make a connection to Columbus and still arrive in time to salvage our meeting. As I gazed at the monitor and made these rough calculations, I heard a woman's voice behind me, calling my name.

"I suppose you heard your flight's canceled," said Lori Overstreet in a tone that displayed a small hint of anxiety. Lori was Jay's girlfriend. She hated for Jay to fly, as much for fear of his safety as the fact that young couples newly in love can't stand the idea of being apart. "I think they're putting you guys on another flight."

She started to say something else, but at that moment I looked up and saw Jay Ramsdell at United's international ticket counter, where agents apparently were tending to customers unseated by Flight 1614's cancellation. He motioned for me to come over.

There, the ticket agent explained the reason our 7 a.m. flight had been scrapped. The night before, she said, a maintenance crew in Philadelphia had discovered a mechanical problem with the plane that was to fly to Denver and become our ride to Chicago. The good news was that there were, indeed, several more flights from Denver to Chicago. The bad news was that the first three, the morning flights we hoped to catch to ensure making easy connections and a timely arrival in Columbus, were full. It was July 19, the middle of summer, and vacationing families arriving early to check baggage had apparently beaten us late-arriving business travelers to the punch. The agent put us both on stand-by for three morning flights and got us confirmed seats on a 12:40 p.m. departure. She checked our bags through to Columbus and told us they'd probably arrive well before we did. We'd both flown stand-by before with success. We decided, standing there in the terminal contemplating our immediate futures, that we liked our chances.

By now Lori, who'd driven Jay to the airport to see him off, needed to leave for work. I told her good-bye and said I was going to wander over to check another flight information monitor to confirm our itinerary. This was not true at all, as I'd written everything down at the counter, but it seemed the considerate thing to let these two say their farewells in privacy — what little there was in the middle of an airport terminal. Still, I didn't want to be in the romantic cross-fire of two people who were absolutely crazy about each other.

Jay and Lori had been a couple for several weeks at the time I took the job as Jay's deputy commissioner and their relationship seemed to grow stronger and stronger by the day. To hear Jay talk, it sounded as if they spent virtually all of their free time together. One anecdote summed up their relationship perfectly. They'd been on a weekend trip to Durango, in beautiful southwestern Colorado, when they happened by a pet store and saw a fluffy Samoyed for sale. They couldn't get over how cute the dog was, and the next day they rushed back to the store to buy it. But the dog was gone, already sold. So when they returned to Denver, they found a farm outside of town where the owners raised Samoyeds and bought one. It lived with Jay, but I vividly recall when they brought the dog to one of our softball games and Lori toted it around as if it were their baby.

"Go to Daddy," she would say.

"Go see your Mommy," he would say.

Everyone laughed at their silliness, but also envied their unabashed affection for one another. It reminded me of the way people should be when they're love-struck.

All of these things flashed through my mind as I watched Jay walk Lori to her car, and I couldn't help but think about Diane and our great marriage and how good life had been to me, too. I had not yet reached 30, and had never contemplated becoming deputy commissioner of anything. Yet here I stood, making twice as much money as I'd ever made before in a job that kept a former jock-turned-reluctant-lawyer close to a game he loves, helping to run a league that was only a heartbeat away from basketball's big show.

***

My father sold feed to South Dakota farmers for more than 20 years, barely eeking out a living, it sometimes seemed. My mother worked at a variety of jobs over those years, including as a secretary, store clerk and later a real estate agent. Somehow, they managed to raise seven children and make ends meet.

I can't classify our family as poor, but it was amazing how tight things were financially. I grew up in the town of Madison, about 50 miles northwest of Sioux Falls, the largest city in the state. As the children of simple, hard-working parents, I and my six siblings were handed down clothes, baseball gloves and the simple philosophy that a person's worth lay in his character, not his paycheck.

There were few rich people in Madison, at least in the economic sense. But we played ball, swam, golfed, shot firecrackers and lived life in an atmosphere that, while chronologically the '60s and '70s, now seems a cultural throwback to the '50s. On a hot summer day, we could take off on our bikes for a day's adventures and our parents would never worry about our safety. We never locked our homes or cars. Ever. For role models we never had to look beyond our own families, and that's where I found the two most important influences on my life — my older brother, Jeff, and my father.

From my father I learned a Midwestern work ethic that nurtured the idea that I could achieve anything if I applied myself with grit and determination. Although this did not turn out to be quite true in all cases, my athletic career being a case in point, the lesson has applied to every real career opportunity that has presented itself.

My father and I always were close and we shared a love for the outdoors, particularly hunting and fishing, that allowed us to spend a fair amount of time together. And some of the greatest moments I have ever had with my dad occurred when we simply sat and talked. One such moment unfolded in the kitchen of our house, when I was a sophomore at Madison High School playing four sports like most of the other boys in our class of 163. My dad and I happened to be talking football, about our high school team. Out of nowhere, he spoke words I can't ever forget. "Just between you and me," he said, "I think you're going to be one of the best quarterbacks ever to play at Madison."

His words were almost shocking. First of all, they were sincere. My father didn't deceive his children with false flattery. And second, as a 150-pound athlete, I didn't exactly inspire comparisons to Bart Starr or Johnny Unitas. But I felt my confidence surge with my father's words, which still mean so much to me even now. After missing my entire junior year because of a broken collar bone that occurred two days before our first game, I started at quarterback my senior year and enjoyed some success. I don't know that I was one of the best ever to play quarterback at Madison High School, but I had one good year. Fortunately, during that season, we happened to have an outstanding football team and I was surrounded by great athletes who virtually guaranteed my success. My father helped push me to the limits of my natural ability and I wound up helping the team to a great season, but I know it could never have happened without the guys who played around me.

The most influential athlete in my life, though, was my brother Jeff. Jeff had tremendous natural running ability. No doubt propelled by the work ethic instilled by our parents, he became a world-class middle distance runner, ran four sub-four-minute miles in college at Kansas State and barely missed qualifying for the 1976 Olympic trials. His success and the attention and admiration that went along with it captivated me. I resolved to seek that same level of achievement and figured that baseball would be my sport, as it required no great size or physical strength.

When I went off to college at South Dakota State University I played on the baseball team. But after two years I transferred to Washburn University in Topeka, Kansas, where the baseball atmosphere was a few notches more intense. There, I found myself playing around guys who'd been drafted by major league teams and decided, at about age 20, that I really wasn't all that far away from the big time. I'd always hit well, but my defense at shortstop and second base left a little to be desired.

In the summer after my junior year I attended a tryout camp hosted by the Cincinnati Reds. In the morning, the first thing the coaches did was time us in the 40-yard dash, which I ran fast enough to earn a call-back for the afternoon session. The next test was a simple throw to first base from deep in the shortstop position, the longest throw an infielder normally has to make. They rated my arm below average. One of the coaches, being brutally frank, told me that I'd never have a major-league arm. Although I appreciated his honesty, it brought an end to my pro sports aspirations and also put an asterisk by the work ethic handed down through my family. Sometimes, determination and hard work are not quite enough. A generous dose of natural, raw talent never seems to hurt.

So I finished my playing career at Washburn with the satisfaction of having maximized my athletic potential and graduated with a degree in communications in 1982. Then I enrolled in the university's law school and served as an assistant baseball coach during the three years it took me to get my law degree. Just as I started my second year of law school, an opportunity to do color commentary on the Washburn football and basketball radio broadcasts opened up. I'd done some high school games in the previous years, calling them for free just to get the experience, but this Washburn gig was an actual job — if you can call $20 a game plus travel expenses real compensation. A year later, I moved up to the position of play-by-play announcer. I was the "Voice of the Washburn Ichabods," which seemed like a pretty big deal at the time. The experience, at least, paved the way for another broadcast opportunity, calling basketball games and doing marketing work for the Kansas City Sizzlers of the Continental Basketball Association.

From there I felt poised to jump to the next level of pro sports, but once again I learned that determination and work ethic — and even the fair level of radio talent I'd developed over the years — weren't always enough to move ahead. I'd applied for four major college play-by-play positions, one National Football League announcing job and three National Basketball Association openings and not only failed to land a job, but also failed to rate a single interview. Still, I determined that basketball was my best sport and made an NBA job my professional priority, even as I hung out my shingle and started a law practice in Topeka.

Becoming a lawyer had never seemed an end in itself so much as a means to reach other goals, a valuable tool and an attractive line on my resume. But there I was, practicing family law, doing collections, taking whatever I could get my hands on or whatever the other three established lawyers with whom I shared office space happened to throw my way. The trial work was fun, not entirely unlike athletic competition in terms of preparation and performance, but the desire for a sports broadcasting job still burned bright.

In the summer of 1988, a series of events created a domino effect among NBA broadcast positions and left an opening in Indiana, which needed a radio play-by-play announcer for the Pacers' games. I sent an audition tape and resume to Larry Mago, the team's director of broadcasting. We did a telephone interview, which I thought went well. Near the end of July, as I returned to my law office from a child custody hearing, my secretary told me that "Larry somebody from the Indiana Pacers is on the phone." He had promised to call whether or not I got the job, and despite the secretary's nonchalance I knew this was a moment of truth for me. In the anxious moments before I punched the blinking light on my telephone, I hoped for two things: First, that I'd gotten the job; second, that if I hadn't, I'd be able to handle the rejection.

"Jerry," said Mago after an exchange of pleasantries, "you didn't get the job. You were close. You were really close. You're an excellent announcer."

I hung up expecting to have to fight back tears, but there wasn't much sting to this rejection. Mago had been kind and professional in his explanation of why I hadn't gotten the position and he seemed sincere when he said that I was an "excellent announcer."

I left the office early that day to go for a five-mile run through the streets of Topeka and clear my head. Although Mago's encouraging words still echoed, my next course of action seemed clear. I was thinking about giving up the sportscasting dream, at least for the time being, to move in another direction. I didn't feel so much that I'd lost my career path as that I'd been directed to a detour. When I laid this all out for Diane that night, her response relieved so much of the pressure I'd felt. Do whatever makes you happy, she told me.

After a few more weeks of consideration, I resolved to look for new opportunities that might combine my experience in sports, law, marketing and broadcasting. But since I'd already signed on to do my fourth season of Sizzlers broadcasts, I decided to see that through while I looked for other options. I wasn't quite ready to throw in the towel on the radio front, but I felt that it couldn't hurt to loosen up my arm a little. Even with an eye now toward expanding my horizons, I knew in my heart I would someday come back to sportscasting. There was no question about that.

Meanwhile, some major changes were happening in the CBA's front office. The commissioner resigned and Jay Ramsdell, then the deputy commissioner, was poised to ease into the vacancy. I had met Jay three years earlier when he was president of the Maine Windjammers team and I was working for the Sizzlers, and we'd become good friends. Jay was only 24, but already he'd begun to make his mark on professional sports. It seemed outrageous that such a young man could find himself in charge of a pro sports league of any description, but Jay was no ordinary young man. The team owners let him run the show on an interim basis for four months. In that short period of time, he sold them completely on his abilities. It had occurred to me that if Jay did get the commissioner's job, perhaps I should inquire about the deputy commissioner's position. When the owners officially made Jay the youngest commissioner ever in pro sports, I sent him a letter asking whether he might consider me for the deputy opening.

I didn't hear anything from Jay for a month and was ready to write it all off as wasted effort when the telephone rang one night at home. It was Jay, asking me if I remembered sending him the letter. I'd thought about it every day since mailing it, but I tried to be cool. He said he wanted to hire me, contingent on an OK from the owners, which was basically a formality. There were no sham interviews, no "We'll seriously consider you as a candidate" or "We'll get back to you." The job was mine if I wanted it. And I did. I think Diane was as excited as I was. Two days later, I called Jay and accepted the offer, which involved moving after the season from Topeka to Denver, where the CBA was headquartered. Diane and I found a townhouse and I started work that spring, on April Fool's Day, 1989.

I started the job feeling excited, but not without some apprehension. I wondered if Jay would turn out to be the amazingly efficient, if unconventional, wonderkind that he'd seemed during the previous three years I'd known him. I wondered if it would be uncomfortable, working for a man I not only respected professionally, but also considered a close friend. It took about two weeks to dissolve those anxieties. Jay was the genuine article, the same irrepressible personality that presided over a meeting of the league's owners as ran an informal staff meeting in our CBA offices.

At the time I started my new job, the league playoffs were underway and I spent a good share of the first month and a half on the road, either monitoring playoff games or tending to league business off the court. When the playoffs ended, Jay and I made two more trips together. The first was to the World Basketball League all-star game in Las Vegas and the second to Pensacola, Florida, where we spent three days trying to iron out some ownership problems with the franchise there.

The next trip on our agenda would be Columbus, Ohio, the site of the CBA's 1989 player draft on July 20. Most of the office staff flew in on the 18th while Jay and I stayed behind and put in a productive day's work in the relative quiet of our near-vacant headquarters. At about 3:30 p.m., Jay wandered into my office and we talked about the upcoming draft. He had some concerns about the television production and so we decided to meet with the TV people as soon as we got to Columbus the next day. Around 4:30 Jay poked his head back in my office and said he was taking off and that he'd see me first thing in the morning, when we were to catch our 7 a.m. flight. On the way out, he said good-bye to our administrative assistant, Susie Malin. She couldn't have realized the finality of his farewell.

***

When Jay Ramsdell and Lori Overstreet finished their long goodbye outside the airport terminal, he and I decided that since the next flight to Chicago wasn't scheduled to depart for another two hours we'd grab some breakfast. Jay had a favorite dining spot on Stapleton's Concourse E, a sparsely used extension of the terminal that was quite a hike from the United gates. But we figured we had plenty of time to kill, so what the heck.

I thought about calling Diane but decided against it, at least until our travel plans firmed up. So we found the small restaurant and I ordered a chocolate croissant, which sent Jay into hysterics for reasons I don't understand to this day. But that tiny detail made the meal memorable, partly for Jay's laughter with almost every bite I took and partly for the conversation between the chuckles.

Although the exact topics remain a blur, I'm fairly certain we talked baseball and, Jay being the dyed-in-the-wool New Englander that he was, eventually got around to hashing out the fortunes of his beloved Boston Red Sox. We chewed on that until about 9 a.m., when we figured we ought to check our fortunes as stand-by passengers. I stopped at Gate 14 on the B Concourse to check on Flight 142, the 9:29 departure, while Jay proceeded to Gate 18 to check on Flight 262, which had a scheduled departure of 9:30. Our strategy: If one of us discovered two open seats, we would run and grab the other. After checking in with the gate agent to make sure our names were on the list, I sat down and waited for one or both of our names to be called. Just minutes before the flight was to leave, the gate agent announced that all seats had been filled. I got up to go see how Jay had fared, but he was already standing in front of me with inquiring eyes.

"Any luck?" he asked, his tone indicating that he'd come up empty.

"Nope," I replied.

Our next chance for escape to Chicago loomed at 10:55. Jay had a membership with the Red Carpet Club, United Airlines' VIP lounge equipped with work stations and telephones, so we decided to head over there and make some calls. My first was to Diane. I explained that so far we were 0-for-3 on flights out of Denver and that, because we were flying standby on the 10:55 flight, I might have to hustle on board at the last moment and not have time to call her. We agreed that it would be best for me to update her on our situation once Jay and I landed in Chicago.

"I love you," Diane said just before we hung up.

"I love you, too," I said.

Around 10:30, Jay and I headed out of the Red Carpet Club and back toward Gate 21, where United 228 would depart at 10:55. Jay checked to make sure we were on the stand-by list and then we played the waiting game again. Ten minutes later, we finally got some action. The public address system called Jay Ramsdell to the counter. He was in. I looked at my watch. It was 10:45. I figured that my own chances of scoring a seat on the flight were slim. A couple minutes later, an announcement confirmed my suspicion by apologizing to those remaining stand-by passengers and urging all those with boarding passes to proceed onto the plane.

At this point, we were running almost four hours late leaving Denver. I knew it was more important for Jay to reach Columbus in time to meet with the TV people than it was for me, and so as much as I enjoyed traveling with him, I hoped he'd simply grab the seat and go.

"Just go ahead," I urged. "I'll catch up to you. It's another two hours until the next flight. I'll just see you at dinner tonight."

"Nah," Jay replied. "I'll wait." His face broke into a smile. "Hey, we're in this thing together, we'll fly together." And with that, he walked to the podium and surrendered his seat to the gate agent. Other than thinking it was a nice gesture on his part, I didn't give much thought to Jay's decision. Since then, I have thought about it often.

We returned to the Red Carpet Club to wait out the two hours until the next flight, United 232 at 12:40 p.m. What seemed an eternity earlier, the ticket agent had assured us both that we'd have confirmed seats on 232, so we settled in to while away the time with a sense of both resignation and relief. Finally, we were a sure bet to get to Chicago. I thought about calling Diane to give her an update, but then realized that our new connection to Columbus would give us 45 minutes on the ground in Chicago; I'd call her then. So at 12:20 p.m. I stepped up to the podium at the gate where United 232 would depart to make sure everything was in order. And it wasn't.

"Mr. Schemmel," said the gate agent, "we don't have a seat for you on this flight. We have you flying stand-by."

Frustration was now turning to anger. I tried to remain cool. I calmly replied that I'd been assured by a ticket agent earlier that morning that I was confirmed on this flight, that I had been waiting over five hours, that I absolutely had to have a seat. The agent never looked up, which was the first indication that my pleas were having no appreciable effect.

"I'm sorry, sir," the agent said. "I show you being originally booked on the 7 a.m. flight, then on stand-by for the next four flights to Chicago, including this one. If you'll take a seat, I'll call your name if we can get you on the flight." I took a deep breath.

"What about a passenger named Jay Ramsdell?" I asked. "I'm traveling with him. What's his status?"

"Mr. Ramsdell has a confirmed seat."

The foul-up would have been comical if it weren't so irritating. The first time Jay wound up with a confirmed seat while I came up empty was sheer coincidence. This time it was a simple mistake. I took another deep breath, weighing the relative merits of an angry, emotional appeal or a more reasoned approach. I decided to try reason, hoping to get through to the agent that one of her co-workers had screwed up and now I was paying the price.

"I'm sorry, sir, there's nothing I can do," she said. "If you'll take a seat in the waiting area, I'll call you up if there is a seat."

As I turned away from the ticket counter, dejected and disgusted, Jay approached. He'd arrived at the gate a few minutes before I did and also learned that United had mistakenly put me on stand-by. The agent had told him there was another flight to Chicago leaving at the same time as United 232 at the very next gate. It turned out that flight, too, was full, but Jay took the initiative of putting me on stand-by for that one as well. For the millionth time that day, I looked at my watch, which read 12:30 p.m. We positioned ourselves on the concourse so we could hear public address announcements for both gates. Almost immediately, I heard a sound that floated on the air like music.

"Mr. Schemmel, please come up to the podium."

The wait had ended with the fifth attempt to board a flight from Denver to Chicago. Jay and I would fly together. We would make our connection to Columbus. We would get the television problems ironed out and the Continental Basketball Association draft would proceed the next day. After five hours, we were finally leaving. It had been a frustrating morning, to say the least, but all the trouble and misfortune seemed behind us now. What more could go wrong?

I actually felt particularly fortunate when I realized that no other stand-by customers were called after me. I was the last passenger to get a seat on United Airlines Flight 232.

THE
EXPLOSION

We walked down the ramp toward the jumbo-jet, a United Airlines DC-10, with a sense of relief, though probably looking a little worse for wear. One of the flight attendants, Susan White, walked with Jay and me and seemed to pick up on the fatigue that had settled over us during our nearly six-hour wait to catch a plane out of Denver.

"I hope you guys don't plan on getting any sleep on this flight," she said with a smile. "There are a bunch of families with us today with lots of kids, so good luck trying to get any rest."

"Are you kidding?" I said. "We're just thrilled to be on the flight."

Jay and I were indeed on the flight, but the cancellation of our original flight to Chicago appeared to have wreaked havoc on all of the succeeding flights. We were flying together, which was Jay's intention when he turned down his stand-by seat on the 10:55 departure, but the redistribution of passengers stranded by that early-morning cancellation made it impossible for us to find two seats together. I ended up with a boarding pass that assigned me seat 28F. Jay was in 30J.

Nearly everyone else had been seated by the time we boarded the plane, so we were able to move quickly through the aisles to our seats, which was good because it was already 12:40 and a flight attendant had issued the routine instructions for all passengers to be seated so the aircraft could move away from the gate. But as I looked down the aisle to zero in on the empty seat that would be mine, my relief evaporated into another cloud of frustration. Just when I figured my problems were finally over, another one presented itself. Seat 28F was taken. I couldn't believe it.

Walking toward my assigned seat, I could see that it was occupied by a boy, perhaps eight or nine years old. I glanced at my boarding pass to make sure it wasn't me who was mistaken. I stopped next to the row that contained my seat, but before I could say anything, a middle-aged man sitting next to the boy spoke up.

"Do you have 28F?" he inquired, a little sheepishly.

I told him I did, as politely as I could, trying not to let my frustration show.

"This is my son," the man continued in a friendly tone, nodding at the boy on his right. "He's supposed to be in 23G. We'd like to sit together. Would you mind taking 23G? It's an aisle seat."

"Sure," I replied. "No problem."

Then I turned to find my new seat, half expecting it to be filled as well. That seemed to be the way my luck was running. But it wasn't, and I welcomed the opportunity to sit on the aisle, which I preferred anyway, and let the father and son be together. When I plopped down in 23G, the thought occurred to me that I'd never been happier to sit down in an airplane in my entire life.

I looked around to find Jay, who'd originally been seated just two rows behind me. The main cabin of the DC-10 seats nine across before tapering off at the rear of the plane. As one faces forward in the cabin, there are two seats on the left-hand side, an aisle, five seats in the center section, an aisle, and two more seats on the right side of the plane. In 23G, I was on the inside edge of the right aisle. Now Jay, in 30J because the seating alignment skips the letter "I," was seven rows behind me in a window seat on the right side.

I glanced at my watch, which showed 12:50 p.m., almost six hours since our original flight was to leave. It took another 25 minutes for us to negotiate the taxiways and sit in line behind other planes, but at 1:15 we were on our way. Finally.

Shortly after take-off, I decided to do a little extra preparation for the CBA draft the next day, partly to familiarize myself with the college players who would be chosen and partly just to while away the time before we hit Chicago on the dead run to make our new Columbus connection. I read through the information packet our media relations staff had compiled and looked up occasionally to see the famous sportscaster, Jim McKay, narrate an in-flight television program on horse racing, a sport in which I have next to no interest. His fatherly face, his smoothly authoritative voice and that special on horse racing seemed inconsequential to me at the time, but they apparently burrowed into my subconscious, only to surface in the months and years later as elements of a recurring nightmare.

Finally, the combination of the video and the work before me, no doubt augmented by the stressful morning, put me in the mood to recline and relax. I dozed, though for how long I'm not sure. I awoke to the sound of flight attendants moving their way through the cabin with a lunch cart. No longer was I in the mood to sleep. I realized it had been a long time since the chocolate breakfast croissant that had made Jay roar with laughter, and hunger now took hold of me. It was time for lunch.

The flight attendants called it a "picnic lunch," an easy-to-eat menu of chicken strips, potato chips, an apple and a cookie. I remember thinking that, in the middle of the summer when families travel with children, it was a nice marketing touch by United. Kids all around me seemed to be enjoying the meal. And contrary to Susan White's half-joking prediction of crying babies as Jay and I boarded the aircraft, the children all seemed happy and well-behaved as we cruised through clear, smooth skies. For the first time all day, I felt completely relaxed. That peace was loudly and rudely interrupted a few moments later.

The sound seemed to come from behind me — not an unusually loud pop, or a bang or a boom, but an explosion. Short but thunderous, it echoed through the cabin with a shock, both physical and emotional, that caused me to sit bolt upright in my seat.

Almost simultaneously, the plane seemed to drop slightly. It was not the sudden drop that sometimes tosses a plane in choppy air, but an easing drop, a drop that seemed to have more to do with suddenly diminished capabilities of the aircraft than any influence of weather or even clear-air turbulence. These suppositions raced through my mind and yielded a frightening conclusion: We were going down.

Knocking my empty coffee cup over on my tray table in front of me, I grabbed the armrests of my seat. It was probably more of an emotional brace than a physical one, as simple logic would have revealed the futility of trying to secure myself at

34

36,000 feet for a virtual nose-dive. The slow drop continued and my vision of impending doom became more and more vivid.

Although we were not free-falling but more or less easing downward, I imagined us easing right into the farmland below. News coverage of Pan Am Flight 103, downed by a terrorist bomb over Scotland just three months earlier, flashed before my eyes. So did Diane's face. I don't know if I actually spoke these words or formed them silently with my lips, but in my mind I was talking directly to her. "I'll miss you, sweetheart. I love you."

My grip on the armrests remained fierce when suddenly the downward movement of the airplane seemed to change just slightly. We were banking to the right. Oh no, I thought, we're going into a spin.

I heard a woman scream, giving voice to a fear that remained caught in my own throat. My heart pounded so hard that it seemed my entire body throbbed. Then it suddenly occurred to me that I hadn't breathed in the several seconds since the explosion and downward pitch of the DC-10. But my efforts to find a breath were unsuccessful. My coffee cup, already knocked on its side, rolled with the right-hand bank of the plane until it plunged off my tray-table and into the aisle. Somewhere behind me, a child cried out for the first time since we'd boarded the plane.

It might have been another few seconds — time seemed suddenly irrelevant and impossible to gauge — before the idea hit me that not only was I going to die, but all of us in this aircraft were tumbling toward the end of our lives. Curiously, I found myself trying to figure exactly how many people were on board. But more screams interrupted the calculation.

What had it been, 30 seconds since the explosion? My hands were still glued to the armrests and the pounding in my chest was unrelenting. My mind, whose circuits went haywire in the immediate wake of the explosion, returned to thoughts of Diane and gave shape to the notion that I would never see her again. Those thoughts, too, were interrupted — not by more screams but by the physical sensation that we were coming out of our drop. Indeed, we were leveling off.

My grip on the armrests finally started to relax, though my heart was not so easily convinced. Pain shot through my chest while my breath returned in quick bursts that slowly, gradually, grew deeper until they felt almost like sighs. The throbbing that started with my heart and spread to the farthest extremities of my body finally began to subside, but the adrenaline rush had been only slightly slowed down by these vaguely comforting developments. We were not dropping. The feel of the movement of the aircraft seemed normal again. But I was not convinced. Something was still wrong. We were banking to the right.

Still taking the deep breaths in an effort to relax, I became sensitive to every pitch and shudder of the aircraft as I tried to understand what was happening and where we were headed. I listened for more clues, trying to remember what the plane sounded like a minute ago, before the explosion. My ears strained to hear the engines through the sobbing that now replaced the screams of seconds before. The engines sounded different, but I could not describe exactly how. Intermittently, the plane would shake as we continued to bank to the right. Something clearly was wrong, yet we were still flying.

I'd never been a terribly religious person. The Catholic mass I'd attended as a kid always seemed the longest hour of the week and, even after marrying a decidedly more spiritual person in Diane, my own spiritual side usually remained in the closet where it could, on occasion, be retrieved for emergencies. Now, though, I prayed.

Strangely, my first of many prayers that day was not a prayer for deliverance. It was a prayer of thanks. I would repeat it several times over the next 44 minutes. I thanked God that Diane was not with me. I thanked God that my wife did not have to share this terror.

***

I always like to tell people, tongue in cheek, that Diane and I met the old-fashioned way — in a bar. A mutual friend introduced us in the spring of my junior year at Washburn. Diane was two years younger, shy and not particularly athletic, and in many ways quite the opposite of me. That might have been exactly what drew me to her, once the physical attraction had pointed me in the right direction.

Initially, we didn't seem to have that much in common, but I remember being impressed by her commitment to family that became obvious even in our casual conversations. That would become the cornerstone of a relationship that grew steadily once I got the nerve to call her about a week after our introduction.

We dated over the following summer and I began to realize that Diane hid nothing of her gentle personality behind any kind of false front. She was simply herself from the beginning: caring, soft-spoken and, true to our first meeting, very family-oriented. After about a year of dating, marriage seemed less a question of whether as when. We didn't spend a lot of time talking about it, but we both seemed to know instinctively that we were on a course to spend the rest of our lives together. For me, this was more than a little ironic. After spending a childhood clothed in hand-me-downs and with so very little money for anything, I'd looked forward to the day when I'd graduate, strike out on my own with a good job and enjoy all the social and financial self-indulgence of bachelorhood. Suddenly, shortly after my graduation from law school and Diane's graduation from college, there I was, waiting for her to walk down the aisle. That much in love, I found the call of the wild not nearly so appealing.

We married in 1985. Diane had been raised Methodist and converted to Catholicism after we were married, but by any denomination her religious beliefs and spiritual development were miles ahead of my own. We attended church regularly, but much of the time I felt as if I were just along for the ride. I suppose I moved ahead spiritually from my childhood indifference, but not by much. As a couple, I might have been the stronger personal-

37

ity, but Diane was definitely the stronger person and, as I would later learn, her faith had a lot to do with that.

Diane was born in Torrance, California, a suburb of Los Angeles. When she was four, her parents returned to their Kansas roots and settled in Topeka. She was the middle sibling, flanked by an older brother and younger sister, and her parents were the same kind of hard working folks as my own, though with very different personalities.

She grew up very middle class in a family that never had money to burn and always handed down clothes and toys from one child to the next, just as my family had. Although she lived in a city of about 125,000, Diane seemed more of a small-town girl. Her father, Carl, worked as a custodian in a public school system for years before moving to a job with the Kansas Highway Patrol, from which he retired. Her mother, Peg, who has worked for 20 years in the food service area of the same school district, practically qualifies for sainthood. She devotes most of her non-working hours, it seems, to performing whatever services, large or small, that can make her family's lives easier and happier. Diane has a lot of her mother's traits.

Diane's older brother went to work right out of high school, so she became the first in her family to attend college. She graduated with dual degrees, in business and home economics, but her focus has always remained fixed on family. To that end, we'd always talked about having kids, two or maybe three, and Diane wanted so much to stay home to care for them when the time came, presumably after we'd had a few years of marriage to simply enjoy each other.

We'd never set a rigid timetable for starting a family, but we had a rough idea. Consequently, Diane afforded me the luxury of pursuing a pie-in-the-sky sportscasting career, with all its frustrations and strange twists of fate, while she worked a variety of jobs with no particular long-range goal in mind, settling into whatever fields seemed interesting and presented opportunity at the moment.

Diane had always assumed that I wanted a son as our first-born. I always assumed she wanted a girl. The truth was that it didn't matter to either of us. We just knew that one day we wanted to have a family and, with any luck, have the opportunity to show those kids the same kind of love that had surrounded us during childhood. After four years of marriage, the subject had started to come up more and more in conversation. We felt ourselves gravitating toward that point in life when enlarging the family seemed a comfortable fit. Our marriage had only gotten stronger in the preceding years. Since we'd married right out of school, we'd heard from other couples that our closeness might soon disintegrate amid regrets over never experiencing single life on our own. It simply never happened.

***

As I sat in the DC-10, I thought about the fact that I may never see my wife again, except in my mind's eye, and I thanked God she was safe on the ground in Denver.

When I finished the prayer, I scanned the cabin to see how the rest of the passengers were coping. What I saw was fear, even terror, in their eyes. There was not a contagious sense of panic, just a plane filled with very scared people. I'm certain that if we had lost cabin pressure and the oxygen masks had dropped, panic would have been rampant, lending an even more dire urgency to the situation. But the simple fact that we were still flying, and not plummeting, had a somewhat calming effect. And that calm grew when the captain, Al Haynes, came on the public address system to let us know what was going on. I knew that I needed to listen not only to his words, but to the sound of his voice.

In his first words to his passengers, Captain Haynes told us that there was a problem with the No. 2 engine. He said that it had been shut down, but the DC-10 was equipped to fly with the remaining two engines, though we might be a little late arriving in Chicago.

All around me, I could see people relax and hear their sighs of relief after that first announcement. Despite the captain's assurances, though, I had doubts. We were still in the air, still flying what seemed to be fairly normally, but I had the strong sense something wasn't right. It wasn't that I thought Haynes was being less than truthful or that he might be sugar-coating our plight. It was more a gut feeling that maybe there was more trouble than anyone had figured initially. A few minutes later, Haynes came back on the public address system and confirmed my fears.

In his second message to the cabin, he explained, in the same calm but in-command voice, that the explosion had damaged the No. 2 engine as well as the rear of the aircraft. He paused momentarily, and I became aware of low groans and bursts of sobbing. Haynes went on to explain that the crew was having some trouble flying the plane.

Now the crying seemed to be coming from all around me. Again, there was no widespread panic but a strong sense of impending doom and our own powerlessness. I replayed Haynes' words in my mind again and again, trying to analyze both the content and tone. What was their real meaning? His admission that there had been damage to the rear of the aircraft, coupled with his announcement that the cockpit crew was having trouble flying the plane, added up to potential catastrophe in my mind. His strategy, I was convinced, had been to tell us just enough to make us aware that the situation was serious, while also offering reassurances to keep us hopeful and the panic to a minimum.

Once Haynes had signed off from this second announcement, the flight attendants started preparing us for the emergency landing. None of us were to leave our seats, under any circumstances, they warned. As they quickly gathered the remaining lunch trays, I thought about the pressure they must have been feeling at that moment. While the rest of us were concerned with ourselves and our families, they had to put their own fears aside and ready nearly 300 people for a desperate attempt to land a crippled aircraft. Again, I prayed. "Help them, God. Please help the flight attendants."

Georgia Del Castillo was the flight attendant in my area. She delivered instructions calmly and gracefully even though, as I learned later, she had never before prepared a cabin for an emergency landing. We were given two options for bracing ourselves upon impact. If it was physically possible, we could lean forward and grasp our ankles. If we preferred, we could cross our arms and grab the top of the seat-back in front of us and wedge our forehead into it. To me, the second option seemed more secure. We were told to locate the nearest emergency exit and instructed to keep our shoes on, but leave jackets, briefcases and purses behind when we evacuated the plane. We were to exit by sliding down the emergency chutes. No matter what happened when we landed, we were told, the crew would use the chutes to get us off the plane.

When the flight attendants had finished giving us the first set of emergency instructions, I looked at my watch. It read 2:35 p.m. I'm not sure why I did what I did next. It might have been reflex or force of habit, or perhaps even subconscious wishful thinking. Since I'd grown up only about 120 miles from Sioux City, I knew we had moved from Mountain Time to Central Time. So I moved my watch ahead one hour. This was something I always did when I traveled. Diane always kept her watch on Denver time, no matter where we were, but I liked to be in tune with the local schedule. That it would occur to me to do this aboard a plane that might very well be headed toward disaster — fixing my watch as if time, in the big picture, really mattered — probably indicated only a nervous attempt to fill the frightening emptiness before touch-down.

It had been 20 minutes now since the explosion, and each minute stretched out as if it were elastic. Crying still echoed around me, but it seemed softer. I prayed again, the same prayer

I'd offered earlier, thanking God that Diane was not with me. So many times I'd traveled and wished that she could be sitting in the next seat, but this time I felt a sense of joy and relief that she was not. There was also a sadness rooted in the firm belief that I would never see her again. Diane and I had had two conversations that day and both had ended with us saying we loved each other. We hadn't parted angrily. We hadn't parted with any unresolved feelings. Under the circumstances, that was no small comfort.

Then, I began to take inventory of my life. I had two wonderful parents and six siblings, all of whom, in their own unique way, had been inspirations in my life. I had a great marriage to a woman I adored. I'd worked my way through college and law school, started my own law practice and taken a pretty fair shot at climbing the sportscasting ladder. Then I'd landed the job with the CBA. I felt like I'd done it all with hard work. No one had ever handed me anything. And I had done it all, I felt, without compromising myself, and without cheating or hurting anyone else in the process.

My life was basically in order, at least as much as anyone has a right to expect when suddenly faced with death. "Take me, God, if you have to," I prayed calmly and silently. "I'm ready."

As I tried to focus on significant regrets in my life, I was surprised when nothing really leaped out at me. But there was one thing I'd left undone that seemed not so much a regret as a sad realization. I would never be a father.

I sat in my seat and closed my eyes. I thought about all the things I would miss by not experiencing parenthood. I would miss watching and participating in Diane giving birth to our child. I would miss holding the baby in my arms and rocking it to sleep. I would miss teaching my son or daughter to ride a bike, tie a shoe or hit a baseball. I would never hear someone call me "Daddy." I thought about never having the opportunity to shape my own child's life in a positive and productive way. It all sounds so cliched now, but at the time the very thoughts tore at me. I leaned forward in my seat, covered my face with my hands and cried.

It wasn't that I felt Diane and I should have started a family sooner. It wasn't a regret over missed opportunity. It was more a dawning of how much parenthood really meant to me, how I'd been anticipating it deep down so very much. I wanted to live for that. I wanted to live to see the miracle of birth and experience the love for my own flesh and blood. But I was convinced I would not.

As the minutes edged on, I felt little fear. I thought about the after-life the way everyone who ever thinks about death probably fantasizes about what it holds. I thought about meeting the twin sisters I never knew. Four years before I was born, my mother gave premature birth to two girls, both of whom died a few hours later. Meeting two of my sisters for the first time. I actually felt a twinge of anticipation.

My thoughts drifted back to Diane. I wondered how she would cope with my death, and whether it was good or bad that we hadn't had children. I wondered if she'd marry again and find happiness following the tragedy that was about to unfold.

I prayed again, asking God to watch over her and take care of my wife. I prayed that prayer over and over, convinced at that moment that I would never see her again.

Chapter

4

IMPACT

A child's crying brought me out of my trance-like state and back to the reality of the passenger cabin of United 232. When I looked up and to my right, in the direction of the sobbing, I first saw a woman with medium-length blonde hair sitting in the right-hand aisle seat of Row 22.

There was nothing remarkable about this woman, no quirk of physical appearance that would make her particularly memorable. She looked about 40 and was of medium size and build. I noticed her left hand, primarily because she held a wadded up tissue in her fingers and intermittently would turn her head toward the aisle and dab her eyes. She wore a wedding ring on the hand that tried to dry the tears, the tears she obviously did not want a little boy to see. He sat on her right, by the window, and looked to be perhaps seven or eight years old.

I felt transfixed by the drama. The mother kept up her subtle deception for several minutes before the pressure became too great to bear. Gradually, the tears began to fall faster than the tissue could absorb them. Sensing the futility of her effort, she finally gave in to emotion and broke into a mass of quivers and sobs. Seeing the bravery stripped from his mother's face, the boy succumbed to the same contagious attack of fear and helplessness, and tears streamed down his face as well.

Although we'd been instructed not to leave our seats, I thought about defying the order. I wanted to try to help. On the other hand, I didn't want to make matters worse by thrusting myself, a complete stranger, into a moment that seemed so intensely personal. Besides, what could I possibly say that would make things better under circumstances like this?

Still, I sat there debating and feeling slowly drawn out of myself, out of my own concerns about mortality and the laundry list of what-ifs, and into this scene one row in front of me. Then I saw the boy push away from her chest, as if his flood of emotion and tears had suddenly subsided just long enough for reason to kick in. He looked into his mother's teary eyes.

"Are we gonna die, Mom?" he asked.

I couldn't sit still any longer. The boy looked to be about the same age as my nephew Jonathan, Jeff's little boy, who I'd watched grow up with the kind of pride and love I figured would one day be directed toward my own child. For the years that Jeff and I had both lived in Topeka, I'd often babysat with Jon and loved to watch him play the sports he loved so much. So as I watched this young kid on the airplane pose perhaps the toughest question a mother can ever hear, one she prays she never has to answer, I thought about Jon being in that situation. The mother's burden became my own.

I didn't stop to consider whether what I was doing was appropriate, an uncalled-for intrusion or a stranger butting in at the worst possible moment; I only knew I could not sit there and say nothing. So I unbuckled my seat belt and stepped forward into the aisle, coming to rest on one knee next to the woman. I looked past her and caught the gaze of the boy.

I had no quickly rehearsed speech to give because, really, how does one even begin to explain danger and death to a seven-year-old in an airplane falling to the earth? One can't fall back on some soothing thoughts about heaven the way one might in explaining the passing of the family dog to a bereaved child. I certainly couldn't understand and digest all that was happening to me, and there was no way this boy could be talked out of his terrifying confusion with last-second appeals to logic, philosophy or theology. It was a desperate moment and I did the only thing that seemed to make sense. I lied.

"We're not gonna die, buddy," I heard myself say to him. "I'm a pilot and I know we'll be OK. I've flown planes before that have lost engines. These kinds of planes are made to fly normally when an engine goes out. We'll be just fine."

I am certainly not a pilot and what I know about airplanes you could write on a match-book cover. But the boy did exactly what I had hoped he would do. He stopped crying.

Maybe this was the truth or maybe it was just my own wishful thinking, but much of the fear seemed to fade from his face. At the time, I thought that the mother, too, had bought into my improvisation. Thinking back today, however, I believe she almost certainly knew that I'd made the whole thing up.

For a long while afterward, those lies weighed on me. Part of me would argue that I was only trying to help, yet another part argued back that it wasn't fair to be so untruthful and that there must have been a better way to handle the situation without being dishonest. But when I stood up to head back to my own seat, the mother touched my arm. "Thank you," she said calmly. I think she knew exactly what I was trying to do.

It seems an almost insignificant exchange now, considering the scope of the tragedy of the crash of United 232, but I still wonder, every once in a while, if I did the right thing. And to this day, I don't know the identities of the woman and the boy — and their very presence seems almost mysterious. Although the flight was full, the airline records don't list anyone in those two seats. Perhaps families separated by last-minute seat assignments had moved around once on board. That might have accounted for some minor confusion about who was sitting where. But in the days after the crash, I checked every newspaper I could get my hands on, filling in names on a seating chart as locations of victims and survivors were made public, and never did learn who might've been sitting there, and whether they lived or died. I have called United Airlines many, many times over the years and posed the question of what happened to those two passengers, but no one has ever been able to give me an answer. I asked a surviving flight attendant who was seated nearby and she remembered the seats being occupied, but had no specific recollection of the individuals who sat there. It was the same with other survivors in that general area of the airplane to whom I spoke later.

Whoever this woman and boy were, I hope they made it. I'd like to talk to them again. I'd like to apologize. I'd like to tell them I'm sorry I lied, and hope they understand that I did so with good intentions.

At 3:45 p.m. we were about 15 minutes away from touchdown in Sioux City and I spoke to one more passenger. Kevin McCarthy, who looked to be about my age, late twenties or maybe early thirties, sat immediately to my left. On his left was his wife, Jaqueline. We'd been on the plane for more than an hour and a half, yet, amazingly, this was the first time Kevin and I made eye contact. He spoke first.

"Can you believe this?" he said, in a tone that sounded more like the mild irritation you'd expect if we'd been needlessly delayed on the runway.

"It's something, isn't it?" I responded, my question sounding like an equally ridiculous understatement.

It wasn't sparkling conversation or packed with deep hidden meaning. It was two guys in a life-or-death situation who simply didn't know what in the world to say to the stranger seated next to them. Although we exchanged no more words, I couldn't help but think about what must be going through Kevin's mind. There he sat living the one monumental fear that I'd been spared: His wife sat next to him, enduring identical fear, uncertainty and turmoil. Once again, I thanked God that Diane wasn't with me.

Several times since the explosion I'd turned in my seat and tried to catch Jay Ramsdell's eye, but always without success. Now I turned again to look at him and, once again, we did not make eye contact. He was speaking to the passenger next to him, probably a lot more intelligently than I had in my nervous exchange with Kevin.

Meanwhile, the plane continued to make right turns. There was a slight bit of unusual vibration and shaking, but for the most part the sensation was one of a fairly normal flight. Then again, knowing that something had gone terribly wrong and put us in grave danger made the smooth movements of the plane all the more eerie.

As I tried to imagine what was going on in the cockpit, a flight attendant approached and spoke to a man seated one row in front of me and one seat to my left. He nodded at her words, unbuckled his seat belt and followed her back toward the front of the cabin. A few moments later, a woman of Asian descent and her young son, who looked around two years old, appeared in the aisle and slid in to sit where the man had been sitting. The flight attendant followed them, carrying pillows that she then placed all around the toddler while explaining that he would need to sit on the floor during the landing, between his mother's legs and buffered by the pillows. Like any typical kid that age, he wasn't interested in sitting still. He stood up in his mom's lap, peered at me over the seat back and grinned.

The vision of this boy's precious face, beaming with a toddler's innocence, made me forget for a split-second where I was and what was about to happen. But I never would forget that face. I learned later his mother's name was Sylvia Tsao. The boy was Evan, age 21 months.

Twice now the flight attendants had briefed us on emergency landing procedures, so all that was left was the waiting. My meandering stream of consciousness slipped into prayer once again. Then, for some reason, my mind wandered to the practical aspects of our landing. For most of the last half-hour or so I'd been preparing myself for death, rummaging through the inventory of my life and making sure I had peace with God. But suddenly, I wasn't quite so sure that my time was up. Maybe, I thought, just maybe, I wasn't going to die.

Maybe panic had gotten the best of me and caused me to think desperate thoughts about my demise. Maybe the odds were not so horribly stacked against me. Reason overtook grim resignation.

The same compulsive need for organization that had prompted me to reset my watch to Central Daylight Time now moved me to consider the different crash scenarios that might unfold. Or maybe it was just the former high-school quarterback, instinctively diagraming a Hail Mary pass play in the dirt. I would probably die in the crash, but just in case I didn't, I wanted to be ready. Don't panic, I told myself. Stay calm. Help other passengers out of the plane. Don't flee the aircraft.

Those thoughts were interrupted by Captain Haynes, back on the PA system. He was reminding us that he would give us a command — "Brace! Brace! Brace!" — in about two minutes, which would be about 30 seconds before landing. He didn't pull any punches. "And folks, I'm not gonna kid anybody, this is gonna be rough," he concluded.

As the extreme danger of our situation hit home once again, I suddenly remembered something — another practical matter that moved me to action. Grabbing my briefcase from under my seat, I opened it and tore off a piece of paper from a legal pad and scribbled a message:

July 19, 1989
> *Aboard United Flight 232.*
> *Whoever finds this note, I have a new life*
> *insurance policy. The papers are in my*
> *guest bedroom closet.*
>> *Jerry Schemmel*

For some reason, I couldn't remember if I'd told Diane about the policy. So I shoved the note back in the briefcase and under my seat. In retrospect, it seemed silly that I didn't stick the note in a pocket, particularly in light of our instructions to leave all carry-on items behind when we evacuated the airplane. I suppose under stress, even when you think you're reacting clearly and rationally, sometimes you can be totally out to lunch. But with that detail taken care of, I mapped out my individual plan for the aftermath of the crash.

I made Sylvia Tsao and her son a priority; I would find them immediately and make sure they were OK. Then I'd help the mother and son I'd spoken to earlier. I checked for the nearest emergency exit, which was between rows 21 and 22, just a few feet away from my seat in 23G.

My mental preparations, finally, seemed to be as complete as they could be. All that remained was the excruciating anticipation. Then, I instinctively glanced over my right shoulder. Jay was looking directly at me. He smiled and gave me a thumbs-up sign. I returned the gesture. I would later come to realize this was our unknowing farewell.

I knew we were getting close. And then the announcement came. Captain Haynes gave us our final instruction, the order to brace. The philosophizing, the preparation, the pondering — all that was over. Everything from here on out would be reaction to the unseen forces that would deliver all of us to our fate.

As I crossed my arms and began to wedge my forehead against the seat-back in front of me, I caught some movement out of the corner of my eye. Sylvia Tsao was struggling to control her son, who had no intention of sitting still among the pillows between her legs. I felt caught between the urge to help and the imminent desperation of our situation, instantly regretting that I hadn't thought to switch seats with the person sitting next to her so I could assist her with the boy. I felt so incredibly helpless. The only thing I could do was pray. "God, please help her," I whispered.

The words were a final admission that the situation was out of my control. It was a strange feeling, one that settled in as we silently counted down the captain's 30 seconds to impact that now seemed stretched well beyond the promised time frame. I glanced to my right, toward the window, not knowing what to expect. All I could see was a bright blue summertime Iowa sky. It seemed so long since Captain Haynes' command. I wondered if maybe at the last minute the captain had decided to make another pass, to bank into another turn and come around for a better approach.

In the slow-motion reality that seemed to precede our landing, I couldn't help but close my eyes and take an emotional look in the mirror, as if to gauge my feelings at that precise moment. It was a strange time to try and step back from all that was happening, but much later it made some sense to me. I needed to know what I was feeling. I needed to make sure I wasn't going to die scared.

I took stock of my feelings, and confirmed that I was content with myself and my fate. Peace was what I felt, peace and calm. It sounds so odd to admit now, but in those final seconds before impact, I felt good. I felt ready for whatever was going to happen.

The wait dragged on: "It's been more than 30 seconds," I remember thinking to myself, and just as the thought formed in my head, we hit the ground.

How do I describe the impact? It felt, for lack of any comparable experience, exactly like you'd expect it to feel if you'd dropped thousands of feet out of the sky and hit the ground. The sound matched the force of the jolt, seeming to come at once from both inside and outside my head. At that moment, there would have been no way to even subconsciously put words to the event, but the feeling in my gut was that this was no crash landing. In fact, this was no kind of landing at all. It was simply an airplane slamming to earth.

For all the painful clutching of the seat-back in front of me, my hands immediately lost their grip and my head, wedged against the same cushion, popped straight up like some character in an arcade game. The irresistible momentum moved me forward and upward from my seat until I had the sensation of floating in the air, held back only by my seat belt.

Gradually, the momentum slowed until I could feel myself easing back into my own seat cushions. Though my eyes were squeezed tightly shut, afraid to look at the havoc unfolding around me, I somehow became aware that the cabin lights went out. Screams cut through the thunderous sounds of the impact. I reached out to brace again against the seat-back in front of me. My hands groped in the darkness but felt only a void; there was nothing there anymore. The seat in front of me was already gone. I tried in vain to clutch something, anything, to help fight the unbelievable force trying to wrench me from my seat. But the crash had instantly rearranged the cabin in ways too horrible to imagine.

With no seat-back to grab, I fumbled for my own arm rests and managed to pull myself back into my seat, as deep into the cushions as I could. For a split-second I felt I was making headway, that I was winning this battle against the laws of physics; and then, in the next instant, I heard more screams and moans. I let my eyes open in the near darkness of the careening cabin and saw a human body fly past me, upside-down. A woman, still strapped in her seat, flew past me on the other side. A storm of debris seemed to whirl around me, as if I were sitting in the eye of a hurricane. When a ball of fire shot past on my right, from front to back of the cabin, I remember thinking it was just a matter of time before something hit me. I ducked my head and tried to cover my face. For all my mental preparation for this moment, there was nothing left to do but react instinctively to the raw physical chaos. It was a helpless feeling, a sensation of total vulnerability.

Once again, time moved in slow, elastic increments. The plane, too, seemed to be slowing slightly, though in reality it was still screaming across the ground at a frightening clip. But there was a steadiness to the motion, and the thought occurred that the worst was over, that we would simply coast to a stop and — miracle of miracles — I might even walk away from this experience. That's when we flipped over.

A sharp pain rippled through my back as I felt myself, still strapped into my seat, roll forward with the pitch of the cabin. A tremendous burning sensation that started in my lower back and traveled quickly up my spine to the back of my neck made me wonder, momentarily, if I'd been electrocuted.

A moment later, I hung upside-down in my seat, waiting for the momentum of the roll to right us. But it never did.

The burning in my back now moved to my legs as the skid continued in this suddenly disorienting world of reverse gravity. My hands slipped hopelessly from the armrests and I dangled down, toward the cabin ceiling. But my seat-belt somehow held firm. Still sliding upside down, I tried to imagine what had happened to me, what had caused the pain from head to toe. The thought flashed through my mind that I perhaps I had broken my back.

The slide seemed endless, but just like the moments before, I sensed again that our motion was somehow stabilizing, and that we would eventually grind to a halt. Then came another jolt, a sharp pain that exploded in the back of my head and triggered a bizarre flashback to a high school football game 12 years earlier. My Madison High School team was playing its homecoming game against Watertown High, when an opponent had blind-sided me with such unexpected impact that the hit knocked me silly. For that brief moment in the cabin of the plane, I saw the face of a teammate, Kerry Pearson, and our head coach, Dean Koester, looking down at me as I lay on the grass turf at old Trojan Field in Madison. As I began to drift back to reality, I figured that some flying object had finally hit me in the head, but seconds later I realized that this, too, was an illusion. The plane had come to an abrupt halt, so suddenly that my head had slammed back into my own seat.

I was still upside-down when the plane came to rest. The next moment I was standing up, with no detailed memory of how I managed to unbuckle the seat-belt and ease to the floor — which was actually the roof of the cabin.

For all the introspection, philosophizing and planning that consumed the minutes leading up to the crash, the aftermath was ruled by basic instincts. In the darkness, I stood there calmly wondering if I was dead or alive. These thoughts were not dressed up with the drama we sometimes associate with dying. The idea of God, and the possibility that I might now be primed for an introduction, did not cross my mind at that moment. There was no scanning the blackness for some bright light that I would follow to eternity or whatever might be awaiting me. I simply and calmly wondered: Dead or alive?

Unable to detect any blood on my clothes and numb to the pain that had been shooting through me just seconds before, I sought the answer. And it came in the form of more pain, sharp and sudden, that caused my right hand to recoil. I looked down to see fire shooting at me from a wall of debris The fire had burned my knuckle. I was alive.

Slowly, my eyes adjusted to what remained of our portion of the cabin, lighted mostly by flames. Where I had minutes earlier made note of an emergency exit stood twisted, burning steel.

Where Georgia, the flight attendant, had been sitting there was only a wall of fire. "She's dead," I thought. "Forget about her. Move on."

For the first time since impact the concept of death, the reality of human casualties, hit home — though I would later learn that Georgia had survived. The horrible toll struck me much more vividly as I turned and scanned the rest of the cabin. Even in the dim light and gathering smoke, the scene was shocking.

Dozens of people remained strapped in their seats, still upside down. Some were struggling to break free. Others were hanging limp and lifeless. From one dangling passenger, blood trickled to the floor. From another still body, it poured in a steady stream. And from yet another lifeless form, an arm hung by a thread while flames consumed the rest. Bodies were strewn across the ceiling, now the floor of the airplane. Some moved. Many did not. Seats had collapsed, row by row, and been flattened. Yet, incredibly, shadowy figures also moved about, on their feet, in the smoky light. That scene, that first conscious glimpse of what United 232 had wrought, would never go away. It would appear over and over in nightmares.

No sunlight illuminated the interior of the wreckage. I could see only by the light of the fire. And through the smoke and fire I could see no exit. What an irony, I thought. Here I had survived a crash in a jumbo jet but now would die in the aftermath, either by the suffocating smoke or the fire or both.

I tried to gather my wits. I told myself to concentrate on one task — help the others — and perhaps in the process I could find a way out. "Forget the dead," I had to keep telling myself, though forgetting would be impossible. "Help the others."

Silence and thick, black smoke dominated the cabin. Choking from the smoke, I looked for a blanket or pillow, anything to place over my nose and mouth, but with no luck. Finally, I simply cupped my hand over my face and began moving around the cabin, not sure whether I was heading toward the front or rear of the plane but always moving toward the shadowy figures of other survivors.

One woman lay on the floor and I helped her sit up, and then saw that one of her legs was badly broken. Still, she seemed alert and calm. I helped an elderly man unbuckle his seat belt and eased him to the floor. His face was almost completely covered with blood, but he kept repeating that he was OK. And then, reacting to the sound of a woman's voice, I turned to see a shaft of light — sunlight — pouring into the cabin. Already, people were moving toward the opening in the fuselage and disappearing into the light of day, even as the gathering smoke and intensifying flames intermittently obscured the passage. That was our exit. There was a way out. I knew at that moment I was not going to die. I knew then I would be a survivor of flight 232.

There was an amazing sense of calm, of order, to the impromptu evacuation. Two middle-aged men stood next to the hole, methodically helping the small gathering of passengers make their exit. I joined the process, handing off one woman to the two men when I spotted another woman heading the wrong way — away from the sunlight and back toward the thickening smoke and flames. When I grabbed her arm, she turned. It was Sylvia Tsao, the woman who'd been sitting one row in front of me, desperately trying to control her restless toddler as we made our final approach. Now, she was alone, and the terror in her eyes had nothing to do with self-preservation.

"You've got to get out," I said, trying to sound as calm and authoritative as I could. "The opening is this way."

"No! No! I can't find my son! I can't leave without my son! Please, you've got to help me find my son!" she answered hysterically. "Please help me find him!"

I hesitated before answering, trying to weigh the dangerous reality of the moment against the maternal instinct that would not let this woman leave the wreckage. The flames were growing more intense by the second. I knew there was no time to reason with her.

"I'll find your son," I blurted, "but you have to get out yourself. Now."

Whether or not she argued, or even responded, I can't recall. The next thing I remember is leading her quickly to the two men at the opening to the outside. Seconds later, I saw her step into the sunlight.

I knew that there was little or no chance of my finding the boy in the cabin. It was my hope that someone else already had taken him out. Mine was another lie told in desperation, a promise without merit but one spoken with good intentions. In the face of this life or death situation, it did not seem wrong at the moment and, in retrospect, still looms as the only reasonable option under the circumstances.

I had told Sylvia I'd find her son, and I didn't. For awhile, guilt outweighed reason for me as I struggled with the idea of one day facing Sylvia Tsao and being called to account. But finally, the obvious futility of the situation — a burning plane, a cabin rapidly filling with thick smoke and a tiny passenger who could have been almost anywhere in the wreckage — let me come to grips with my decision to say what I said. Sylvia Tsao had to get out of the wreckage or she was going to die.

Moments after I'd led her to the opening, I realized there were no more survivors waiting to exit. I saw one of the men who'd been helping people out move through the hole himself. There was no one left to help, at least that we could see now that smoke and fire had overtaken the entire cabin. I looked at the other man who had been helping people through the opening. His name was Michael Martz, and he later became a member of the U.S. Olympic Equestrian team for the 1992 games in Barcelona.

"Let's go," he said calmly.

He went through first, while I took one last look into our portion of the wreckage. I thought about Sylvia Tsao's boy at that moment. "Look for him," I thought. I surveyed the cabin one time, but saw only dense smoke and chasing flames. I had to get out. I stepped past the encroaching fire and through the opening.

Going through that opening seemed like a passage to a whole other world. Brilliant light, the rays of a bright afternoon sun in Iowa, blinded me momentarily so that my first real perception of the outside came not from my eyes, but from my feet. It was the feeling of the earth giving way gently to each step. Then, the faint smell of the soft dirt seemed familiar and finally, as my eyes adjusted to the daylight, I realized that I was indeed in familiar surroundings. I had walked through dozens and dozens of them in my life, in South Dakota, hunting pheasants. I was in a cornfield.

As my vision cleared, I saw the man who'd come out just ahead of me waiting a few feet away and, it seemed, poised to take off running. Then the thought struck me: The burning plane was going to explode. At least, that's the instinct that perhaps too many hours in front of the television now activated. It happens every night on some program: The burning wreckage, the hero sprinting from the scene. And then, just as he reaches a safe distance — boom! — a fireball erupts behind him. But now, with a burning plane just a few yards away, the possibility suddenly seemed all too real. So I took off, struggling to find traction in the loose dirt and determined to put distance between me and the plane before it exploded. But I didn't get far.

After only a few steps I heard a sound that stopped me in my tracks. It was a human voice, a muffled cry that could only be a baby. And clearly, it was coming from inside the wreckage.

What I did next — head back into the burning plane — would be seized and exaggerated by the media over the following months and years into something remarkable and heroic. But at that moment, there was no weighing of options or gauging of danger. There was no clear realization of risk that might have resulted in a conscious decision to act heroically. There was no premeditation. A baby's cry of distress strikes a chord in every human ear, and I simply happened to be within earshot.

As I wheeled around and headed back toward the plane, the man just ahead of me, who I'm sure could not have heard the cries himself, must have thought I was crazy.

"No!" he shouted. "We've got to go!"

"There's a baby!" I screamed back.

I can't recall much of the next few seconds. I obviously followed the sound of the crying and reentered the wreckage. I really don't know which direction I went or how far into the smoke my steps took me. I know I couldn't see anything and I do remember homing in on the cries. "Keep crying," I remember saying to myself. "Please, keep crying."

I kept moving until I seemed to be standing right over the cries. Feeling the floor in front of me with my hands, I realized that the child was buried beneath debris. I grabbed whatever lay between me and the sound. Because of the smoke, I could see nothing. It was now completely black inside the cabin. I pulled away what felt like a duffel bag. Then a blanket. Then a large piece of metal. That opened up what appeared to be a hole in the floor — really the ceiling of the upside-down plane — that I would later guess to be an overhead storage compartment. I reached into the hole, grabbed an arm and lifted the child out. I held the child's head to my chest, pressing its face against my white dress shirt so as to try to keep the choking smoke away from the infant's nose and mouth.

I don't remember anything about getting back out of the plane. The next thing I recall is stepping back into the cornfield and running away from the wreckage. The thought of an explosion returned and I didn't break stride until my distance from the plane began to feel comfortable.

Perhaps 50 yards away from the downed plane, I stopped to look at the child. It was a little girl in a light blue dress. She had stopped crying and I scanned her tiny body for signs of injury. I saw none — no blood, no abrasions, no burns. There was only a small cut beneath one eye. She didn't seem to be hurt but there was no way for me to know for sure — at least not until she confirmed my diagnosis with a big, beautiful smile.

I resumed my movement away from the wreckage, now at a brisk walk, but had no idea where I was headed beyond the vague idea that this must be the same general direction others had traveled when they left the plane. Finally, I reached a small clearing in the cornfield where a narrow patch of weeds had interrupted the crop. About a dozen people sat, stood or laid there and it was clear they weren't part of any rescue team. They were fellow survivors.

I recognized the woman I'd seen on the plane with the badly broken leg, the woman who'd seemed so calm despite her injury. Now, as everyone's adrenaline began to subside, reality settled in. She moaned with pain. Still clutching the baby, I knelt down between her and another woman holding her hand.

"She's got a broken leg, I think it's best not to try to move her," I offered.

"OK," said the woman holding her hand. "I'll stay with her."

I stood up and looked back toward the plane, which the tall corn hid from my view, and saw only billowing smoke. Glancing in the opposite direction I saw a grove of trees shading a small, white building where another group of people milled about. For the first time since the crash, I thought of Jay Ramsdell. I figured — hoped — that he was among that group. I then turned my attention to the survivors around me and noticed a young woman standing apparently uninjured just a few feet away.

"Would you please take this baby?" I asked. "I don't know who she is or where her family is. I just grabbed her from the plane."

61

"Sure," she replied, as she took the calm infant.

And with that, I headed back through the cornfield toward the wreckage — for what possible reason I do not know. Maybe I thought I'd unconsciously heard or seen something as I made my way from the plane and felt the need to check again for anyone who might be hurt and struggling toward the clearing.

I ran all the way back to the wreckage, or at least as far as I could go. The flames were completely consuming what I now realized was just one portion of the cabin. I couldn't get within 20 feet because of the intense heat.

Staring at the burning shell I had just moments earlier exited, I could feel my entire body trembling, as if a chill had come over me. "My God," I thought, "where's the rest of the plane?"

Chapter

5

THE

WONDERKID

The faces bobbed along next to me, faces that sparked no glimmer of recognition. Some were streaked with blood, others remarkably unscathed. We moved almost as one, through a small clearing that we all assumed led the way out of the cornfield's tall, green maze.

I stopped at the sight of an elderly man lying on his back, moaning in pain and with blood covering one side of his face. I asked him where his pain was coming from, although my medical expertise was roughly on a par with my piloting experience. And like those strange moments in the cabin when I created sheer fiction to soothe a scared young boy, this moment left me with the same empty sensation that comes from wanting to help in a situation I was ill-equipped to handle. I had no idea what I would do or say if this man actually shared his pain, which he did.

"My back," he groaned. "It's my back. Please help me sit up."

I wasn't sure it was a good idea to move a victim with a back injury, but the immediate concern of alleviating his pain made me reluctant to refuse his wish. With the help of another woman who'd separated from the group and stopped to help, I put my arm behind his back and very, very gently pulled him forward. He screamed.

"No! No! Please lay me back down!" he gasped.

And so the woman and I lowered him ever so slowly onto his back once again, into a position that seemed to make the pain more manageable. For some reason, I got the idea to put something under his neck for support. The next thing I knew, I was rolling my suit coat into a make-shift pillow. I placed it gently under his neck.

"Perfect," the man sighed. "I'm just going to lie here for awhile. Thank you. I'll be all right."

"OK," I said. "But you'd better not get blood on my new jacket."

It was a crude attempt at humor, but in the immediate aftermath of the crash, it didn't seem so inappropriate. At any rate, the words slipped out before my brain had time to consider whether a man in serious pain might consider the joke the least funny one-liner he'd ever heard in his life. I felt a sense of relief when the injured man, with his eyes squeezed closed, managed a broad smile. I found out about a month later that the man did not suffer any serious injury. And, incredibly, about a month after that, my suit coat arrived at my house in a box, completely cleaned.

My eyes shifted to another scene. Only a few feet away a man knelt beside a nun who sat, looking somewhat stunned, in the weedy clearing. If I had, in fact, been dreaming this entire sequence of events, then this woman in her black and white habit would have made for an interesting point of analysis. As a student in Catholic grade school, I'd been taught and disciplined by nuns for five years, and their unique effect on my formative years has never been forgotten. I've always carried with me a certain fondness for the unselfish women who make up these religious orders and I try to make that long-standing appreciation known even on chance meetings.

In a dream, or this variety of nightmare, the injured nun might have stood for something deep-seeded, like my own dormant spiritual life suddenly jolted awake. When I squatted down beside her and asked if there was anything I could do for her, she clutched her rosary before she replied.

"No," she said. "I'm not hurt. I'm fine. I just want to sit here and rest. And pray."

In retrospect, she seems symbolic for that phase of my spiritual condition — stunned but not seriously injured, needing time to rest and rejuvenate while seeking some serious answers from a higher authority. Sister Mary Viannea was 77 at that time. She was returning home to Chicago on United 232. In the smoky blackness of the cabin she had seen what looked like a small opening and thrust her hand through it, perhaps not so much an act of desperation as an act of faith. Someone grabbed it and pulled her to safety. This nun, sitting among weeds, fingering her rosary and repeating familiar words — "Hail Mary, full of grace..." — was turning to God for strength.

Looking away from her, my eyes locked on another injured passenger and two men who were attending to him. The men were dressed in military fatigues, and after the second or two it took to realize the significance of their clothing, I knew that rescue workers had arrived. Suddenly, the combat fatigues seemed to be everywhere, swarming the area.

I continued to wander ahead through the clearing until one of the rescue workers started to guide me back toward the runway. In our disorientation immediately after the crash, those surviving passengers from our section of the plane apparently had wandered deeper into the corn, away from the rescue effort.

My continuing compulsion to check my watch revealed that it was now 4:30 p.m., about 30 minutes since the crash. Much of that time seemed a blur, but when the rescue worker finally guided me back to the runway, I once again faced one of those crash scenes that etches itself into memory and never really fades.

Pieces of airplane, slivers and slices of the DC-10 I had boarded in Denver, lay strewn across the landscape. White blankets covered the bodies of some who hadn't survived. The flashing lights of fire trucks and ambulances dotted the scene like daytime fireflies. One helicopter landed on the runway as another took off. People moved in all directions. In keeping with the longstanding cliche, it looked like something right out of a movie — which, of course, it eventually would be.

As the adrenaline rush that had drowned out the immediate trauma of the crash slowly began to subside, the feeling of unreality also started to recede. But my memory of standing on the runway, surveying the physical and emotional wreckage, contains so many blank spaces that counselors would later explain that some of the images might have been blocked as a sort of mental health reflex.

I do remember seeing, in the middle of the runway, five or six seats tangled together in a heap. As I got closer, I realized there was a young girl, perhaps eight or nine years old, still strapped into one of the chairs. Then I noticed a woman in the seat next to the girl. I ran over to them, thinking that no one had yet noticed them. Moving closer, I saw red tags attached to both passengers' wrists. They had been found, and their deaths noted.

If there are other dormant memories of the runway scene, they have never come back to me. The strongest images remain those of emerging from the cornfield to witness the incredible scale of the destruction and then later getting into an ambulance. As one of the ambulance attendants conducted a cursory check-up before I climbed into the vehicle, I remembered the excruciating pain I'd felt right after impact, the pain that shot, white-hot, through my legs and back and left me thinking I might have broken my spine or, perhaps, been electrocuted. For the first time, I realized that the pain, the physical anguish I had felt, was gone, and had been gone from the moment I freed myself from my upside-down seat and began exploring the smoke-filled segment of fuselage that somehow had delivered me safely into the cornfield.

"I'm fine," I told the rescue worker.

Minutes later I began to understand that this was far from the truth. As the fog in my head lifted, reality gradually made its presence felt. A different pain was approaching. I felt tears coming — finally, inevitably. Then I felt an arm draped around my shoulders followed by a gentle hug. Marlis Dejong, who worked as another one of the ambulance attendants, must have seen something in my eyes, something reflected in their glassiness. Suddenly, my tension eased and the tears held back.

The ambulance made its way toward a building that housed the Iowa National Guard. Ambulance workers told us that this had been designated as a holding area for survivors who weren't seriously hurt, although all of us eventually would be taken to a hospital for closer examination. When the vehicle stopped and I stepped again into the brilliant sunlight of a summer afternoon, I saw a large one-story building buzzing with activity. It was only then that I dared to think about my friend.

Jay Ramsdell would be inside this building, I told myself, and that thought propelled me through the door and down a short hallway toward the sound of many voices. Someone was saying that, miraculously, more people had survived the crash than had died in it. I clung to that thought as I reached the end of the hallway, turned to my left and entered a large room holding perhaps a hundred people, most of them seated on the floor along the walls. Quickly, I scanned the room hoping to lock eyes with Jay, but he simply wasn't there.

That could have meant anything. It could have meant he was still in the cornfield, or on the way to a hospital, or anywhere in the mass confusion to which the rescue effort still tended. But I was suddenly overcome with a feeling that was more than a feeling. It was something like an intuitive sense that settled into the pit of my stomach with sickening certainty. My best friend and colleague was dead. I was sure of it, as sure as I had ever been about anything in my life.

I leaned against the wall and slumped to the floor. There was no comforting arm around me now. Putting my face in my hands, I cried for the first time since impact.

***

In November of 1995, more than six years after the crash, I once again stood in Sioux City contemplating why things worked out the way they did. I was getting ready to give a speech about my experience in the crash to the women's basketball team at Briar Cliff College, where I had arranged to meet Jay Ramsdell Sr. We were both in town for the annual Continental Basketball Association exhibition game to benefit the scholarship fund that honors his son.

I had agreed to fit the Briar Cliff speech into my schedule and Jay Sr. had expressed an interest in hearing my presentation, so we decided to rendezvous at the campus. As I headed toward the meeting, I felt a mixture of eagerness and apprehension. Probably the strongest pangs of survivor's guilt hit me when I stand face-to-face with Jay's parents, whose loss far exceeded the devastating void that I felt after his death.

I can't help but wonder what must go through their minds when they see me, when they see the man who worked for the same fledgling pro basketball league as their son, walked onto the same airplane, heard the same explosion and counted down the same terrifying minutes to the same unfathomable impact, yet walked away as their son could not. Do they look at me and think: "Why is he here instead of Jay? Why was he chosen for survival when our son perished? What right did he have to just walk away, with hardly a scratch, while we're left to mourn a young man no less deserving of God's grace?" Do those thoughts live for a moment, for the blink of an eye or the time it takes to shake hands, whenever they see me? Does their personal warmth keep some measure of anger hidden below the surface, where it won't wound or offend?

These were all thoughts that troubled me as I headed toward my meeting with Jay Ramsdell, Sr. I knew the thoughts were patently unfair. Jay's family, and Jay Sr. and his wife, Linda, in particular, had never been anything but kind and gracious, yet guilt remained for me an undeniable force in their company. If they did not look at Jerry Schemmel and wonder why him instead of their son, then I looked at them and wondered for all of us.

When I finally saw Jay Sr., we hugged. And then we cried. Any misgivings I'd had about the meeting seemed to wash away with the tears. Although I still felt self-conscious about giving my presentation on the crash with him in the room — and, in fact, on my way to the podium I briefly considered eliminating some details out of deference — I decided at the last second to change nothing. To my relief, Jay Sr. afterward expressed his sincere approval.

The benefit basketball game that night provided a wonderful yet bittersweet backdrop to my memories of the rising young sports executive who never lost his appreciation for the fact that these are kids' games, and that presented in their purest form touch an innocence and passion in all who bother to watch them. For all the innate talents Jay Ramsdell brought to the job, that appreciation had formed the bedrock of his success ever since he was a kid growing up in Mount Desert, a small town on the Maine coast. Jay's parents had both been prep sports stars, but they passed on a gene rarer than raw physical ability to their son. He seemed to have been born with vision far beyond his years.

At 11, Jay published his own neighborhood newspaper. At 12, he moved on to producing a nationally distributed fan newsletter devoted to the Boston Red Sox, the one professional sports team to which he pledged unconditional allegiance. A year after that, he caught a break at a local high school basketball game, when the radio play-by-play broadcaster needed a statistician on short notice. The announcer asked some students if they knew of anybody who might be even remotely qualified to fill in. The kids looked at each other and replied as one:"Jay Ramsdell."

As always, his work was phenomenal and quickly gained him a reputation in the area. About 60 miles away, a Columbia Falls businessman named Morrill Worcester had put together the Maine Lumberjacks entry in the struggling Continental Basketball Association and soon sought to add the 13-year-old stat whiz to his payroll as the assistant director of public relations. Jay was enthusiastic about the possibility, but also realistic enough to point out to Worcester that he wasn't old enough to drive. Fortunately, Linda Ramsdell was never far behind her son with an encouraging word. "We'll get him to your games," she told the owner. "This is your man." And she was true to her word, driving him roughly 125 miles, round-trip, almost daily during the season.

Linda Ramsdell was right about another thing also: Although her son was still a baby-faced teenager, he was already a man in terms of his ability to accept responsibility, rise to every new challenge and earn the respect of those who worked around him. Inevitably, it now seems, Jay took over as the team's director of public relations and began charting his career course in professional sports.

When he graduated from high school, Jay fixed his sights on the higher education offered not by college, but by the CBA's league office, located in Philadelphia at that time. It was a time of intense growing pains for the league, which had a long and storied history as the Eastern League before expanding geographically and ultimately negotiating a mutually beneficial relationship with the NBA, which essentially had no "minor leagues" to develop players who'd used up their college eligibility. Jay worked as the CBA's director of operations for three years, and in that short span accomplished some monumental feats — nevermind that he was still only 18 when he started.

His organizational skills always had been impeccable, and that trait shone through in Jay's development of the league's first-ever uniform operations manual, which served as the first real quality control for the widely scattered franchises whose motto once could have been, "Anything goes."

Teams often had shaky financial underpinnings; one actually folded at halftime of a game. Attendance sometimes could be counted as easily by sight as by turnstile count and players in the wide-open spaces of the West were known to endure month-long road trips covering thousands of miles — all traveled by van. Jay helped change all that. He set game schedules that made sense, organized player drafts, gave birth to the league's first computer network and, to say the least, put out a lot of brush fires along the way.

As if to complete some unfinished business, or maybe bring his career full-circle geographically, Jay then celebrated his 21st year by returning to his home state of Maine to take charge of a new Bangor franchise, which he named the Windjammers.

In 1986, he headed to Denver, where the league office had relocated under the leadership of commissioner Carl Scheer,

71

who'd been brought on board after a long run as president and general manager of the Denver Nuggets. After three years as deputy commissioner, punctuated by the disappointment of being passed over for the commissioner's job when Scheer moved on to head the NBA's Charlotte Hornets, Jay finally got his chance when the next commissioner, Mike Storen, resigned. At 24, he became the youngest commissioner in the history of American professional sports. And he still looked about 16.

Naturally, he was tested, particularly by owners, some of them self-made millionaires, who had trouble buying into the idea that some fresh-faced kid who never even went to college would be telling them how to run their basketball league. What they came to realize, however, was that Jay Ramsdell, who'd seen the league operate from every vantage point from statistician to the front office, not only had the business sense to make the league a success, but also had the kind of integrity and quick wit that allowed him to deal comfortably with even the most unmanageable egos. It did not take the bullies among the franchise owners long to figure out that Jay could not be intimidated. Though he might have seemed under-age, it was they who were usually overmatched.

During the short time I worked with Jay in the CBA front office, one particular incident stood apart as an illustration of his cool-headed tact, selfless devotion to the best interests of the league and razor-sharp sense of humor. One of the owners had tried to make a trade that involved a player who'd been suspended for drug problems. Quite correctly, Jay declared the deal void — a decision that did not sit well with the team owner, who had his secretary call and instruct Jay to be ready to take his phone call at a specified time that afternoon. The secretary also relayed the order that since I was the CBA's legal counsel at the time, I should join the conference call. The call rang through at the appointed hour and the owner proceeded to launch into an expletive-filled tirade. One of the more civil terms he used to describe Jay was "smart-ass kid."

He was playing the intimidation game, counting on Jay to back down in the face of his withering attack. But Jay was typically well-prepared to respond. He cited chapter and verse from both the league's operational rules and the by-laws that gave him the enforcement power to void the trade. His position was clear and his voice never rose above the level of civilized conversation — all of which infuriated the owner even more. "Since you seem to know the by-laws so damn well," he finally screamed in frustration, "then why don't you tell me what section tells me how the owners can fire you." Jay saw this one coming a mile off. "That's Article 33, Section 4, paragraphs one and two," he responded evenly, without missing a beat. The next thing we heard was a dial tone.

At the time, I wasn't sure if I was more stunned by the owner's foul language and utter lack of respect for the league's commissioner or by Jay's finesse in dealing with it. But I felt compelled to tell Jay, in terms not a whole lot nicer than those we'd just heard over the phone, that I thought the owner was a complete jerk who'd just been whipped and put in his place. And I fully expected Jay to agree. But, amazingly, he didn't. Instead of basking in victory, he defended the man. "Try not to hold things like this against owners," he said seriously. "These guys are businessmen. A lot of them got to where they are today by intimidating and bullying people. That's just the way they operate. Try not to take it personally." With those words, I began to realize that Jay possessed not only management skill, but wisdom beyond his years — and beyond mine, as well. He carried himself with quiet confidence, unconcerned about criticism or credit that might be cast his way. Just about the only thing that could send him into the doldrums was a prolonged Boston Red Sox losing streak. The rest of the time he dedicated himself to astounding efficiency. And the relentless pursuit of fun.

We were in Rockford, Illinois, for a CBA playoff game just a few months before we got on the DC-10 to Chicago, and a few of us from the league office went to lunch. As we sat talking after the meal, Jay spontaneously went into his imitation of radio personality Paul Harvey, putting our waitress in stitches and entertaining the rest of the place as well. People at neighboring tables couldn't keep a straight face. Other waitresses and busboys leaned outside the kitchen door to catch the act. Jay could handle upstart owners, run a smooth operation and leave them laughing in Rockford.

NBC's "Today Show" flew him to New York to appear as their "Sports Person of the Week" not long after he'd been named commissioner. I remember talking to him about the honor, but he seemed unaffected by the national media attention. But in an unguarded moment, Jay offered another glimpse of his golly-gee-whiz side, the childlike quality that would occasionally come shining through. "Schem," he said, betraying a glimmer of excitement over his trip to the Big Apple, "you should've seen my hotel room. It had a mini-bar in it."

Linda Ramsdell never doubted that one day her son would occupy an office in New York City. Jay had been brought up to think big and, judging from what he'd already accomplished in his first 25 years, his mother figured that only time stood between him and the office of the NBA commissioner. Of course, that assumed he would remain in the basketball arena.

On the one hand, he seemed to have found his niche. His reign as commissioner saw the league expand to an all-time high of 16 teams that traveled by air to all destinations beyond 200 miles. The CBA set attendance records and solidified a broadcast contract with ESPN that promised even greater exposure. And the league had reached another agreement to assist the NBA in player and referee development. But while Jay could see the Continental Basketball Association's potential and he understood how to realize it, the sport was never his passion the way baseball was. It's true that he spearheaded the effort to computerize the basketball league's business, but it's equally true that with a few taps on the keyboard in his office he could call to his screen the box scores for every Red Sox game dating back for years. And for the weekend after our trip to Ohio for the CBA draft, he had planned a pilgrimage to Cooperstown to see his idol, Boston outfielder Carl Yastrzemski, inducted into the Baseball Hall of Fame. Sports visionary that he was, Jay had made his hotel reservation 13 months in advance.

All of these things were part of who Jay was, yet the recurring theme in his life seemed to be one of youthful exuberance. Poetry has never been my strong suit, but about a week after the crash of United 232, some simple lines popped into my head and I felt compelled to write them down in the hope that others might understand the essence, if not the entirety, of a wonderful friend.

I found that Jay's childlike innocence became a recurring theme, and so I called the poem, "Just a Kid." It was read by the minister at a memorial service the CBA staff had for Jay at a mountaintop garden not far from Denver. Later, I felt extremely honored that Jay's parents, who buried their son next to their home in Maine, saw fit to inscribe his headstone with the same words.

JUST A KID

It's hard to believe what's become of him,
So much is what he did,
He was bold and bright and all grown up,
But still he was just a kid.

He beat the odds by being so young,
And accomplishing what he did,
He followed a dream and found a light,
Even though he was just a kid.

He gambled on a league that should have failed,
He drew and made his bid,
He put out the fires and righted the wrongs,
All the while he was just a kid.

We all ask why, why did he go?
So much is what he did.
We love you, Jay, we always will,
To us, you're still our kid.

***

Chapter

6

AFTERSHOCKS

Sitting on the hard tile floor of the National Guard building, leaning against the wall in a room full of people, I closed my eyes and tried to isolate myself from the rest of the world.

I desperately needed to sort things out and let my tears run their course uninterrupted by the well-intended attention of the rescue workers. In an almost dreamlike state, I mentally retraced my steps from the time I'd rolled out of bed that morning in Denver and stumbled to the bathroom to the scene just minutes earlier, when I'd been running through an Iowa cornfield.

I tried focusing on the individuals who'd been seated around me, imagining what might have happened to them. I remembered that the man who'd been seated immediately on my left, the man with whom I'd exchanged but a few awkward words, had not been there when the plane finally came to a stop. Dead, I figured.

I envisioned the face of Georgia Del Castillo, the flight attendant who'd been in a jump seat facing me when we crashed. It didn't seem likely that she'd survived, either. Once again, I pictured the frantic face of Sylvia Tsao, who had placed her tiny son Evan on the floor at her feet just moments before impact. I knew she was alive. And I knew, with the same kind of certainty that gripped me about Jay's fate, that the boy was dead.

Again and again, I flashed each face I could remember before my mind's eye and tried to determine the odds of their survival. It was a morbid exercise that obviously did nothing to improve my emotional state. Later, I would find out I was wrong about both the man seated next to me and the flight attendant. They had made it through the ordeal. But the fate of Jay Ramsdell, which I knew in my heart, would not be easily confirmed — certainly not until I found a telephone and made a round of checks at local hospitals where the injured had been transported.

As my tears subsided and composure returned, I found myself focusing on practical tasks. It occurred to me that, in addition to tracking down Jay's whereabouts, I needed to make contact with my own family and co-workers, who would certainly be learning of the crash and fearing the worst. By concentrating on the immediate need to find an outside telephone line and let others know I was all right, I was able to shove all other concerns to a corner of my consciousness — at least temporarily. I got up from my seat on the floor and approached one of the relief workers, an older woman who stood pouring orange juice into rows of paper cups. She saw me coming and saw something in my face that made her put down the juice container, gently take hold of my arm and look me in the eye.

"I saw you get out of the ambulance outside," she said. "Are you sure you're all right? Can I get you anything?"

"I'm fine," I said. "I would like to use a phone, though."

"There's one in the office at the end of the hall," she said, pointing down a long corridor, "but a lot of people are waiting to use it. You might have to wait in line a little while."

There seemed to be little choice, so I headed toward the hallway. But after just a few steps something distracted me. It was a solemn voice that caught my ear and the flash of a TV monitor that caught my eye. The television sat on a shelf at another end of the large room, and suddenly the announcer's words began to register. He was talking about a plane crash.

I felt irresistibly drawn to the screen, where six or seven other people already stood watching. Seconds later, I saw what I supposed was a segment of news video that showed a large jet-liner cruising toward a runway for what appeared to be a normal landing, only to begin a horrifying cartwheel that became a picture of smoke, fire and disintegration that, from all appearances, could not have left any survivors.

"What crash was that?" I said out loud, to no one in particular. There was a short silence, as if the others around the TV couldn't believe someone had actually asked the question.

"That was this crash — today," someone finally blurted.

Though I suddenly felt foolish, the more overwhelming sensation that passed over me was one of shock. It simply didn't seem possible that anyone could have emerged alive from the violent collision I'd just seen on a videotape shot by a photographer from a Sioux City television station. The more I thought about it, the more I decided that the man who'd answered me had to be mistaken. There was no way I could have come from that crash. There was no way *anyone* could have survived what I'd just seen. But then the tape was shown again, as it would be tens of thousands of times in the days, weeks and years ahead. And this time my mind was able to put the announcer's voice in synch with what appeared on the screen.

"Here again is the tape of the terrifying plane crash that took place just a short time ago in Sioux City, Iowa. . ."

My jaw went slack and my mind went numb, except for the question that kept repeating itself, and would continue to repeat itself as if sheer repetition could elicit an answer that made any sense: How could anyone have survived?

The few seconds of videotape, which would become *the* most watched piece of news footage in American television history, begged the question that could never be answered to everyone's full satisfaction. In a sense, survival was the core issue of the incident, far more mysterious and complex than the technical questions surrounding how an airplane with supposedly sufficient backup hydraulic systems could have found itself in such a predicament in the first place.

Survivors, as well as friends and relatives of the dead, sought explanations from many sources, both spiritual and practical. Years after the fact, I would even put the question to our pilot, Captain Al Haynes: How could anyone have survived? But I could never hope to find an answer. The best I could hope for was to learn to live with it, to forge a truce with the question. While the television replayed the scene yet again, a man stepped through the small crowd of people gathered around the set and shut it off. I guess that was the best answer any of us could come up with at the time.

The improbable scene I'd just witnessed on videotape quickly collided with the strong probability that Diane, who seemed a lifetime away in Denver, might well have seen the same footage. Again, the search for a telephone became paramount.

Steering myself back to where the rescue worker had directed me, I could already see a line of people ten or 12 deep in the hallway. I'd resigned myself to a long wait at the end of the line when I noticed a door leading off the hall into an unoccupied office. Through a narrow window in the door I could see a small desk and, atop the desk, a telephone. Slowly, I turned the doorknob, expecting it to be locked tight. But when the latch yielded, I slipped inside the office and closed the door behind me, not believing my good fortune.

I picked up the phone and my mind drew a blank. I tried to think of Diane's phone number at work, but it wouldn't come to me. She'd just begun a new job that week and I'd written down the number to carry with me. Unfortunately, I'd left the number in my briefcase, which by now was either junk or ashes. Without the recall of Diane's work number, I figured the quickest, surest plan would be to call my office. When Diane got word of a crash, that's where she would call to find out if the Denver-Chicago flight that went down had been mine. I dialed the CBA office in Denver.

"Oh, my God, Jerry!" came the first words from our administrative assistant, Susie Malin, when she picked up the phone. Word of the crash had spread quickly in Denver, and knowing that Jay and I were heading to Chicago that morning, Susie had called United Airlines and learned that we both had been bumped to that flight. I told her that I was fine, but that I hadn't yet seen Jay. And I wasn't about to share my own unconfirmed, gut feeling that he hadn't made it.

Susie assured me she would track down Diane, tell her I was OK and ask her to come over to the CBA office to be there when I called back later. I hung up the phone and immediately picked it up again. If word of the crash was spreading fast — and that piece of videotape seemed destined for nationwide saturation in short order — then I needed to reach my parents. They traveled a great deal in their business of helping furniture stores conduct liquidation sales, but I'd written the phone number of their latest client, a store in Illinois, on a business card that happened to be in my wallet. I dialed, expecting a store employee to answer. But instead, the next sound I heard was my father's voice, sounding typically pleasant and upbeat.

"Dad, it's Jerry," I said, struggling to inject calm into a voice that already had started to quiver.

"Hey, Jer! How ya doin'?" he shot back immediately, and I realized that he hadn't heard. I hesitated for a moment, working to hold back the emotion that was building.

"I'm not doing so good, Dad."

Awkward, dead air filled the moment as I tried to figure out what to say next and while Dad tried to measure what the silence meant. As it had several minutes before, the enormity of the situation came crashing down on me. I strained to keep my composure, knowing that what I said and how I said it would determine the degree of trauma inflicted on my parents. I tried to choose my words carefully.

"Dad, I've been in a terrible plane crash. I'm OK, though. I'm in Sioux City, Iowa."

It was as if saying it aloud suddenly made it all more real, and less bearable. I felt the tears coming and a sense of uncontrollable despair. When I broke into sobs, I felt guilty at breaking the news this way and then tried to comfort myself with the rationalization that even an adult has a certain privilege of emotional regression in the company of his own parents, perhaps especially a son with his own father. If I was entitled to break down in front of anyone, surely it could be my dad. Catching short breaths, I heard the description come out of my mouth in bursts.

"We tried to make an emergency landing, Dad, but we crashed. . . I got out OK and I'm all right. . . but a bunch of people right around me died, Dad. . . we were in a cornfield. . . the plane burned up. . . Dad, a lot of people are dead. . ."

And that was all I could say. That was all that would come out. My father's response took much the same form as Susie's had back at the CBA office, the same sort of words tripping over emotions.

"Oh my God! We heard there was a crash in Sioux City. . . Jerry, I had no idea you were. . . oh, my God!" And that was all dad could manage.

Those initial exchanges with my father are very clear even now, but both my parents and I do not remember any of the rest of our conversation. There were so many telephone calls to follow, themes repeated so many times, that only the stark reactions remain clear. As I hung up and turned to leave the office, I saw that word of my discovery had spread. Another line of survivors, perhaps a dozen deep, had formed outside the door, waiting to use the telephone.

Back in the main room of the National Guard building, a relief worker told me that a bus would be taking us to a hospital in about 15 minutes. I headed outside to get some fresh air on what remained a beautiful summer day, except for the wail of sirens and the plumes of black smoke that smudged the blue sky.

I walked a block down a sidewalk and then turned back toward the building, just to be moving, just to be going somewhere. As I approached the building again, I saw a man I'd seen in the wreckage during that span of time that seemed long ago and so far away. He'd been helping other passengers escape the fire through a hole in the fuselage and, a few moments later, he had hollered for me to run from the wreckage. We locked eyes in a moment of mutual recognition.

"How you doin'?" I asked softly.

"OK. How about you?"

"I'm fine," I said, not yet realizing that I'd injured my upper back and suffered smoke inhalation.

"Hey," he said. "That was really something with the baby."

It took me a moment to realize what he was talking about: The baby? Then it came to me — the little girl whose cries had sent me back into the wreckage.

In the confusion, the gradual migration to the National Guard building, the breakdowns and the phone calls, I had completely forgotten about the baby I'd rescued and then handed off to the woman in the cornfield. Now I found myself wondering who she was and what had happened to her parents. Later, I would learn that Lori and Mark Michaelson, their seven and

83

five-year-old sons and their 11-month-old daughter Sabrina — the baby I'd found trapped in an overhead compartment — had been on their way to Cincinnati, where Mark was about to start a new job. Incredibly, all five survived the crash.

Like Sylvia Tsao, who'd clung to her son Evan, Lori Michaelson had held Sabrina in her arms until instructions on the intercom advised her to place the baby on the floor of the aircraft and pad her with blankets and pillows. Lori held on desperately after impact, but when the plane flipped onto its back, Sabrina slid out of sight. When the plane finally came to a stop, Lori grabbed one son and made her way forward through the cabin. She soon found Mark, who had the other boy.

"Where's the baby?" Mark had asked.

"I lost her," came Lori's helpless reply.

Mark sent his wife and both sons out the hole in the fuselage and disappeared back into the smoke-filled cabin. Standing inside the wreckage, he could hear his daughter cry, but the noise stopped before he could follow the sound of her voice. Finally, the smoke and flames became overwhelming and he had no choice but to get out of the plane. Some 30 or 40 minutes later, after again finding his wife and two sons, Mark saw a young woman holding the baby. And so the entire family, miraculously, was reunited. I would not know any of this, or even the baby girl's name, until hours later.

From the National Guard building, several in our group of survivors boarded a school bus that would take us to St. Luke's Hospital in Sioux City. Nobody said much on the ride, and when we got off the bus we all seemed to move in slow motion toward the hospital receiving area. I went straight to the registration desk to inquire about Jay, but the woman behind the counter said she had no record of anyone named Ramsdell being admitted. She offered to call Marian Health Center, the city's other major hospital, to see if Jay had been taken there, but when she got off the phone and shook her head to indicate she'd had no luck, the response reinforced my fears that had hardened into something more.

Outwardly, I was clinging to optimism and praying my feelings were wrong about Jay. But hope became more and more difficult to manufacture.

From the registration desk at St. Luke's I retraced my steps to a pay phone I'd spotted on the way inside and called the CBA office again. Diane had made her way there and we spoke for the first time since early that morning, when we had traded I-love-you's. The words we spoke over the telephone escape me now, other than the fact that, like several other phone conversations that day, words ultimately dissolved into tears.

When I hung up, I was escorted to a small examination room to await a check-up. Left alone with my thoughts, I was struck by the first realization that my life might be forever changed by the crash of United 232.

How would I ever get back on a plane after what had happened to me that day? Fear of flying became a given, under the circumstances, and therefore any career that depended wholly on the ability to travel great distances — a career as a National Basketball Association play-by-play announcer, for instance — would be impossible. I had survived, but it was as if my longstanding career dream had been left for dead on the runway at Sioux Gateway Airport. It was enough to bring on more tears, and I sat there wiping them away with a paper towel when a doctor appeared.

I told the doctor I was fine, that I felt no pain and had made it through the ordeal completely unhurt. A quick exam revealed no physical ills of immediate concern, and so I was sent to another floor of the hospital where a large, open room — similar to the one at the National Guard building — had been set up as a sort of holding area for survivors who were not seriously injured.

A glass of orange juice and a small toiletry kit was standard issue here, and I settled in to see what would be the next order of business. In a few minutes, a woman entered the room and asked if anyone was interested in doing telephone interviews with the media. Anything seemed better than sitting around contemplating my own sorry state while I remained unable to get further word on the fate of Jay Ramsdell. And any activity that put me in close proximity to a telephone offered at least the opportunity to do some checking of my own. So I agreed to do interviews.

I wound up speaking with media people from all over the country, non-stop, for about 90 minutes. That's when I told the hospital worker that I'd had enough and turned my attention to phoning around to check on Jay's status. But before I could get back into her office, another survivor had stepped in and embarked on his own succession of phone interviews. Although I'd already answered too many questions and had replayed the incident too many times, I jumped when asked if any of the passengers were interested in going to a local TV station for a live interview.

"If I can use a telephone there, I'll do it," I volunteered.

That day, there was very little accounting for time beyond the moment our rear engine exploded. The 45 minutes before impact seemed to last forever for many of us in the cabin, but flew by for the cockpit crew. The aftermath of the crash moved in slow motion, yet the time slipped away until there I sat in a Sioux City television news studio and realized it was 8 p.m. It had been four hours since the crash.

I found a telephone and began calling in search of Jay while I waited for word on when I'd be needed on-camera. Starting with the two Sioux City hospitals, I checked every possibility I could imagine, including hospitals in nearby Omaha, Nebraska and Sioux Falls, South Dakota. I phoned the airport, where a temporary morgue had been established. I called the United Airlines crisis number. Every call brought the same response: No Jay Ramsdell. It was now more than five hours since the crash and I was told that every survivor had been checked into a hospital.

My gut feeling about Jay's death could not get any stronger. My facade of optimism had worn thin.

I ended up staying at the television station for nearly five hours, most of it spent on the phone. I never did do an interview.

But I did watch as another survivor, Bruce Benham, did a live shot with Ted Koppel on ABC's "Nightline." And I watched as yet another passenger appeared live on the local station, giving a miraculous account of how he and his wife and their three children all survived the crash. The parents had each grabbed one child but the third, a baby girl, remained lost inside the plane but ultimately had been found by another passenger. When a picture of the little girl flashed onto the monitor, I saw Sabrina Michaelson for the first time since I'd handed her to the woman in the cornfield. And then I saw her father for the first time ever. Afterward, someone must have told him that the man who'd found his daughter in the wreckage was there at the TV station, because Mark Michaelson took me aside for what seemed an awkward introduction for him and most certainly was for me.

Neither one of us knew exactly what to say. It's not every day you come an eyelash from losing a daughter. And it's not every day you find yourself in a position to save a life. We were both grateful for what had happened, but visibly uncomfortable. Mark started to cry. I could hardly hold back tears myself. The media people who talked to us afterward asked for an account of the conversation, surely hoping for a typical made-for-TV moment. But my recollection is one of simple awkwardness.

"I just want to thank you for saving her life," Mark said. "You're a hero."

"I don't know about a hero," I replied. "It was just reaction. I just followed the cries."

Mark pulled out a business card and handed it to me, saying he'd be in touch. And he was true to his word. A few weeks after the crash, when Sabrina celebrated her first birthday, the Michaelsons took her picture and sent it to me with a card, beginning what would become an annual tradition so that, even from afar, I might watch this little girl grow and grow.

Past midnight, nearly eight and a half hours after the crash, I was still at the station and still on the phone. And still, no word about Jay. At 1 a.m., the station's weatherman, Tom Peterson, graciously offered me, Bruce Benham and survivor Garry Priest the option of staying at his house overnight. We accepted, but nobody got much sleep. Bruce and I had agreed with an ABC producer to return to the station at 6:30 to be guests on "Good Morning America," so we weren't looking at a lot of down-time anyway, but I managed to spend three more hours on the phone in Tom's dining room when I wasn't lying wide-eyed, unable to sleep, on a bed in his basement.

At 5 a.m. I got up, took a shower and put on some clean clothes Tom had given me. The golf shirt was a bit too large, almost as overwhelming as Tom's generosity. I got back on the phone to continue making my rounds of the hospitals and the morgue at the airport until a limousine, provided by ABC, picked us up at 6:15 to take us back to the station. Bruce and I appeared live on "Good Morning America," which I barely remember, and then I spent another two hours on the phone. Then the limo took me back to the airport, where my brother Jeff was going to meet me once he made the four-hour drive from his home in Topeka, Kansas.

I waited at an airport restaurant with two producers from "Good Morning America," periodically interrupting our conversation to run to a pay phone and make what now had become my standard set of eight calls: six hospitals, the morgue and the United Airlines crisis line. Their numbers were etched in my memory. So were their responses: No information about Jay Ramsdell.

Jeff and his wife, Lori, with son Jon in tow, arrived around noon. Just the sight of family took an incredible weight off my shoulders. We sat in the restaurant for three hours, while swarms of reporters from all over the country swirled around us in search of interviews, yet remained unaware that a survivor sat in their midst. At a time when humor was hard to come by, this passed for high comedy and Jeff, Lori and I took the opportunity to laugh at the irony of the situation. But the laughter didn't last.

It was inevitable, I suppose, that I would be struck hard by a simple fact that I'd been dodging for the last several hours. But now, as I prepared to return to Denver on a private flight United had arranged for me, I came face to face with the truth: Jay could have taken another flight to Chicago. I suddenly remembered that he'd gotten a stand-by seat on an earlier flight and then had given it up so we could fly together. United 232 wasn't his flight. It was my flight. Jeff, Lori and I all cried together.

At 3:45, I gave my brother and his family one last hug and got on an airplane.

It was a strange sensation, walking down the corridor toward the aircraft, one of fear mixed with a strong desire to see Diane again as soon as possible. The longing to see my wife overruled fear. And fatigue trumped them both. As I settled into my seat, I took a deep breath and closed my eyes. The very next sound I heard was rubber hitting runway. Our plane was landing at Denver's Stapleton International Airport. I'd slept through the entire flight. I guess one could say I got right back on the horse — and then fell asleep on it.

Two days later, on a Sunday night, several CBA staffers gathered for emotional support disguised as a cookout at the home of Christy Jordan, who also worked in the league office. Christy's mother, Nancy, one of this world's truly wonderful people, answered when the telephone rang, about an hour after we had assembled. Outside on the patio, I heard the phone ring and intuitively knew who was calling, and why. Three days after the event, Jay Ramsdell had finally been confirmed dead in the crash of United Flight 232.

An aerial view of the crash site shows where the DC-10 first touched down, (top of photo, edge of runway) skidded and where it ended up.

The middle section of the aircraft is where most of the survivors came from.

credit: TSgt Pat Kenaley, 185th Tactical Fighter Group

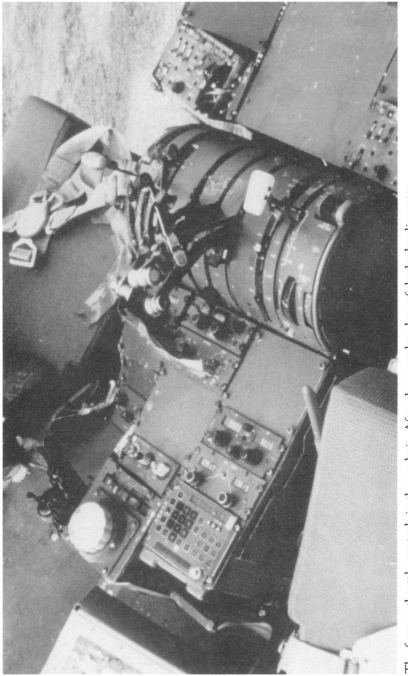

The famous throttle controls in the cockpit. After the complete loss of the hydraulic system, the crew miraculously used engine thrust to fly the crippled plane.

credit: TSgt Pat Kenaley, 185th Tactical Fighter Group

The tail section of the DC-10. Jay Ramsdell was sitting just about where it separated from the rest of the plane.

credit: TSgt Pat Kenaley, 185th Tactical Fighter Group

Captain Al Haynes addresses the media for the first time
following the crash.

Rescue workers attempt to free three crew members, all alive, from what remains of the cockpit. The cockpit was compressed from seven feet to three and a half feet in the crash.

credit: TSgt Pat Kenaley, 185th Tactical Fighter Group

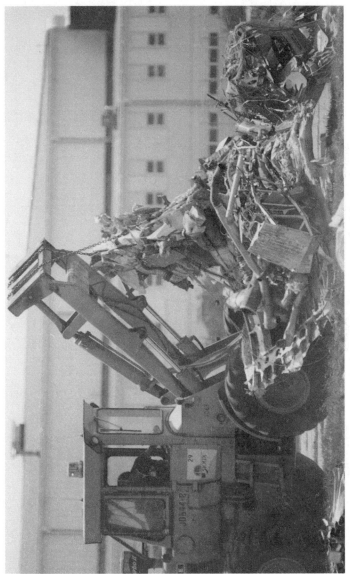

An airport worker hauls away a tangled mess of what remained of the cockpit.

credit: Rocky Mountain News

Rescue workers line up to comb the cornfield. The rescue effort, led by Gary Brown, was phenomenal and later became the subject of a made-for-television movie.

credit: TSgt Pat Kenaley, 185th Tactical Fighter Group

credit: TSgt Pat Kenaley, 185th Tactical Fighter Group

The number three engine lays next to the runway. The number two engine exploded and fell from the aircraft about 100 miles away.

The tail section of the aircraft, the only section that did not burn up, is moved next to a hanger at the airport. It remained there for five years before being sold for scrap.

credit: TSgt Pat Kenaley, 185th Tactical Fighter Group

The charred remains of one section of the DC-10.

The initial impact of flight 232, the right wing hitting the runway, caused a gouge that was nearly two and a half feet deep.

credit: TSgt Pat Kenaley, 185th Tactical Fighter Group

Part of the destructive path of flight 232.

Perhaps the most famous photo from the crash. Spencer Bailey is carried from the wreckage by Col. Dennis Nielson of the Iowa National Guard. The photo was the model for a bronzed statue that was later erected at a memorial site in Sioux City.

Jerry Schemmel during a Nuggets' radio broadcast.

I can't think of too many better jobs than an NBA announcer.

A real family affair. The entire Schemmel group.
Back row: Jeff, my mother Shirlee, my father, Bill, Heidi, Holly.
Front row: me, Jed, Jason, Joel.

Between my girls. With Diane and Maggie celebrating
Maggie's first birthday.

A man and his treasure. With Maggie during a visit to Kansas.

The Schemmel trio in the spring of 1996.

Chapter

7

NOTHING'S
CHANGED

Perhaps the need to manage the trauma of the crash stemmed partly from my upbringing, the simple work ethic that taught me to define a problem and hammer away until it was overcome, and partly from some innate male stubbornness of the same strain that keeps us from stopping to ask directions when we are undeniably lost.

In the weeks and months after United 232 fell to earth, I made several wrong turns, but had neither the knowledge nor the willingness to recognize that I was traveling dangerous, twisting back roads without so much as a map.

My physical condition seemed manageable, and my emotional state, though prone to lapsing into moments of grief over the loss of my best friend and colleague, did not seem particularly crippled when I looked at the big picture. After all, I reasoned, I'd had the composure to deal with countless media requests for interviews, duty that understandably made a lot of survivors uncomfortable as we tried to sort through what had happened to us. The ability to deal coherently with the press had reinforced a sense of strength and normalcy about myself.

Time would move on and I would learn to accept the ordeal, even the unfairness of it all, and proceed with my life and ambitions. Or so I thought.

Although counselors had spoken briefly to us survivors about the chain of emotional events that would probably follow, the advice seemed intended for those among our group who were less equipped to deal with the incident, or those who'd been scarred most deeply by the loss of husbands, wives or, worst of all, children. The therapy, the longer-term issues, the brutal business of redefining families in the wake of such a loss — these were the unfortunate trials to be undertaken by the others, I felt, and my heart went out to them.

Of course, I expected to be struck by certain difficult moments and allowed for these as acceptable fallout from my experience. They were short periods of high emotion that I could understand, even anticipate before I actually felt them, but the most important thing was that they were manageable.

Three days after the crash, Diane and I attended mass at St. Vincent de Paul Catholic Church in Denver. It was our custom to sit near the front, maybe four or five rows back. We were newcomers to the parish, and the circle of friends and acquaintances we'd made aware of my experience on United 232 did not include anyone sitting with us in church. We felt somewhat self-conscious as we, for the first time together, confronted what had happened in relation to our religious faith. For me, it was not a comfortable fit. Though I felt joy at my deliverance and reflexively believed that God ultimately was responsible for it, I could not help but follow logic to the conclusion that God also was responsible for Jay Ramsdell's death and so many others'. As I examined this intense blow to the pillars of my faith, I felt anger blind-siding me like the unexpected hit I took as a high school quarterback.

Diane, of course, was far better equipped spiritually to put my experience in a context that made at least some sense, even if that sense amounted to simply accepting God's will as something totally beyond our understanding and offering humble thanks for the holy mystery of my survival. But I felt dazed and confused, comforted yet disturbed by what I saw as God's hand in the crash. For very different reasons, Diane and I squeezed each other's hands tightly and felt tears streaming down our faces throughout the mass, torn between wanting to cut loose with our feelings and not wanting to draw attention to ourselves. It was a difficult hour, but I managed to leave church feeling that, although I hadn't resolved anything in my first religious communion since the crash, I had at least faced the issue and emerged emotionally intact. I had passed another test and felt vaguely reinforced.

That night, the solid sense of physical well-being that had so puzzled me right after the crash suddenly developed its first cracks. A pain and burning in my chest seemed to grow gradually stronger, and the sensation frightened me in a way it probably wouldn't have if I had felt it right after I'd left the burning wreckage. So on Monday morning, I saw a doctor.

As the doctor stepped into the examination room, I was struck and amused by his appearance — with his reddish-blond hair and thick moustache, he looked exactly like Dan Quisenberry, one of the superb relief pitchers in all of baseball when he played for the Kansas City Royals. We both laughed when I mentioned this and he admitted that, as a matter of fact, many of his patients had told him of the resemblance. Our conversation was moving along almost lightheartedly when he asked me what the problem was, and I told him about the pain and burning in my chest. He asked if I had any idea what might have caused it and I told him that I'd been in the crash of United 232. He sat back in his chair, looking stunned and shaken, though I'm not sure if it was because a survivor of the disaster he'd seen on television dozens of times suddenly stood before him, in defiance of all logic, or if he expected that a dire diagnosis might soon follow.

Dr. Quisenberry, as I came to think of him, suggested that a chest X-ray might illuminate my problem. What he found was the lingering effects of smoke inhalation, and he judged from the fact that they were still so visibly present after four days that I must have taken in a significant amount of smoke while I was still in the burning fuselage of the DC-10. The effects would diminish with time, the doctor said, and there was no need for any kind of treatment other than patience.

He asked if there was anything else and I said there was not, even though my back was still stiff and sore. In my medical wisdom, I assumed it was just the aftereffect of the jolt we'd taken when the plane hit the runway and didn't think it was worth mentioning. Eventually, I would discover that the problem was more serious than that.

The back injury I suffered in the crash, later diagnosed as severe whiplash, would have more lasting effects. I was told certain movements would remain painful even years later, which they did, and limit certain sports and recreational activities like golf and skiing. Cutting back on or even eliminating those two activities was something I didn't have a problem with. It was the orthopedic specialist telling me that I would never be able to run more than a mile or two at one time, because of the pain from chronic stress on my upper back, that saddened me. I loved running. It was my reprieve, my release. And I had always wanted to run a marathon. That, it appeared, had been taken away.

Within a couple days of the doctor visit, still less than a week after the crash, I became more acutely aware of another issue that follows the survivors of commercial airline crashes as surely as the sense of trauma, tragedy and loss. Solicitations began to arrive, calls and letters virtually promising to make me a rich man through the filing of a lawsuit against United Airlines, DC-10 manufacturer McDonnell Douglas, engine-maker General Electric and anyone else who might have deep pockets and some measure of liability.

Sioux City almost immediately was dubbed "Sue City" when the inevitable reality of legal action took off only a day after United 232 came crashing down. The incident happened on a Wednesday. On Friday, the first suit was filed in Illinois state court. By Monday, the first federal lawsuit had been filed in Philadelphia.

As with any other tragedy that begs legal action, the crash of United 232 attracted more than its share of shameless opportunists who were above nothing when it came to playing fast and loose with the ethics of solicitation. Not wanting to appear that it was directly seeking my business, one law firm sent me a mailing disguised as an informational release from a public relations company. Out of curiosity, I called the number listed for the PR firm and reached the switchboard of the law firm. The raw, uncivilized hunger for clients sometimes sank to unconscionable depths. Case in point: One envelope that arrived at my home featured a slick, four-color brochure depicting the lawyer actually standing in front of the wreckage of a plane crash, presumably a tragedy from which he'd managed to squeeze big bucks. So uncontrollably were the opportunists salivating that it's a wonder the envelopes weren't still soaking wet when they arrived in the mailbox.

Still, I opened them and read their contents with a mixture of anger and bemusement, wondering for awhile how the lawyers had gotten my home address and then realizing they'd probably consulted the list of survivors that appeared in newspapers across the country and then simply looked up the only Schemmel listed in the Denver telephone directory. The solicitations served no useful purpose except to drive home the realization that, given the way America's corporate and legal systems operate, some sort of settlement with the passengers (and, in many cases, their families) was not only likely, it was expected — by all sides.

There had been a few moments after the crash when I could feel righteous indignation toward the faceless companies responsible for the engine explosion and, ultimately, the crash. But the anger would recede and I would figure that, given the fact that I was very much intact physically and, after all, alive, I did not have so much to complain about even though, as a lawyer, I was well aware that everyone on board the airplane had a perfectly legitimate cause of action.

When I read about everyone getting attorneys, lining up lawyers to do battle over what promised to be millions of dollars in damages, I weighed my own feelings, still buoyed by the miracle of survival, and decided there was no need for me to do the same. Three reasons came to mind: First, because I had endured a lot less than many of the survivors, I didn't anticipate asking for much in the way of compensation; second, I wanted to avoid actual litigation and figured that reasonable minds could settle the issue without that needless hassle; third, I was an attorney myself, and while not particularly well-versed in this area of law, I felt I could navigate the system adequately enough.

My plan was simple. I would wait until the cause of the crash could be determined, and then contact United and settle the issue, perhaps with no more ceremony than just a few phone calls and a handshake. About two months after the crash, when I received a letter from an aviation insurance company notifying me that it would be representing all the defendants in the case, my decision seemed all the more prudent. For all the criticism swirling around the excesses of the American legal system, this case promised to be as simple as any I'd ever handled, even in my brief career as an all-purpose attorney right out of law school in Kansas.

Still, I did not want to go into the situation blind or ill-prepared, so I researched the settlements of previous airline crashes and tried to put a dollar figure on what had happened to me. It proved a strange exercise — in a way, it's like trying to find the blue book on something that never happened to you before and will never happen again, something that has no market value, something that isn't ruled by the simple laws of supply and demand and depreciation. You might as well try to put a price tag on lost innocence.

There were some tangible financial expenses that followed in the wake of the crash, like doctor bills, but for a person who has basically just walked away from the most harrowing experience of his life, what's left defies description, much less valuation. Serving as my own counsel certainly didn't simplify the process, as a dispassionate accounting of the incident was nearly impossible to render. But I tried, and finally managed to divide my claim into three basic areas. First, there were my physical injuries, which seemed straightforward. The physical part was the easiest to quantify at the time, even if the dollar figure was far too low, owing to my ignorance of the ultimate damage to my body. For the second part of my proposed settlement, the part that gauged the emotional toll, I focused a lot of my effort on the 45 minutes between the time the No. 2 engine blew and our crash-landing in Sioux City, as did all the lawyers working on settlements regarding United 232.

Basically, there were two schools of thought, the most dominant being that the more time that transpired between the first sign of trouble and ultimate impact, the greater the emotional toll on the passengers as we contemplated what surely seemed our impending deaths. This line of reasoning held that where damages were concerned, the meter was running from the time of the explosion: the more time to think, the greater the emotional suffering, the greater the compensation due. The other side of this coin was the position that each minute of contemplation actually reduced the potential award, because it gave passengers the necessary time to make peace with their maker and themselves. Although I stood to benefit financially from advancing the first theory, the idea that our 45 minutes of dire uncertainty somehow was preferable to a hasty nose dive provoked my interest. It prompted me to reexamine the whole incident in search of an answer that came from the gut, not from legal strategy. This was not easy.

The intermittent terror that gripped me throughout our gradual descent could never be recalled with the same crystal clarity of those precise moments. A certain edge was always missing. And so my evaluation of the relative benefit those 45 minutes afforded me was distorted from the outset. Having said that, I had to admit that, as someone who walked out of the plane almost without a scratch, there was definitely some value to the introspection that preceded the crash. Surely I would feel different if the fragmenting fuselage had torn away a limb or produced some horrible physical disfigurement that would follow me the rest of my life. But the fact remained that I was basically intact when I stepped into the cornfield, and ultimately I reached the conclusion that, given this end result and given the option of having the scenario played out in fast-forward mode, I'd choose the prolonged fall from the sky. Of course, it's a purely academic question, something for lawyers and psychologists to argue, because when it matters to us most we never have the choice.

For purposes of the settlement proposal, I figured on the same basis as the other survivors, that when terror and liability collide, time is money. The final part of my damage assessment involved filing a separate case on behalf of Diane, although this did not amount to much in terms of damages. Obviously, I'd survived with minimal injury and her emotional trauma from the incident itself was secondary in nature — although here, too, I surely underestimated the damages as I muddled through the early stages of life after the crash thinking everything was going to be OK.

All in all, it was an interesting exercise, trying to step out of being Jerry Schemmel to become Jerry Schemmel's lawyer.

My dealings with the insurance agent for the defendants were conducted over the telephone, with a crisp, business-like tone. Of course, there was no good reason to expect that the negotiation would be anything else, but without realizing it I still carried some slivers of my other persona — Jerry Schemmel, survivor — into the conversation. I felt vaguely put off by the idea that the voice on the other end of the line did not sound particularly compassionate, though it would be unfair to describe him as ruthless or cold. He was simply a professional, a numbers-cruncher with a job to do, and he seemed intent on carrying out his work with an efficiency that did not leave time for tea and sympathy.

I explained, as professionally as possible, my assessment of the damages and my formula for arriving at what I thought would be a reasonable figure that would keep us out of an extended legal tussle. Perhaps naively, I expected he would quickly concur, maybe even be grateful for my refreshing sense of fairness in contrast to the school of hungry sharks already circling his office. For some reason, I was stunned when he countered with a figure far below my own. We spoke a couple more times over the telephone, but he was surprisingly set in his position. It wasn't going to get done. I knew he and I were not going to settle.

That's when I took a look back at the newspaper clippings that Diane had meticulously begun to save after the crash and found a list of lawyers who represented other survivors. I called Dick Schaden, a Boulder attorney who represented maybe a dozen others with claims from United 232. We spoke for about two hours one day and the next week entered into a standard contingency arrangement. Dick proceeded with a definite eye toward a jury trial and wielded the leverage of multiple plaintiffs.

We filed my lawsuit within a week, but it would be almost two years before we agreed to a settlement. In terms of timing, our filing probably came in the middle of the pack.

Initially, we spoke for two or three hours and I outlined my experience in the crash and what I knew of its lingering effects. After that, we spoke on the phone maybe once a month, when he'd update me on the status of our claim. Other than these brief conversations, there was no protracted legal involvement for me, personally — no depositions, no grilling by lawyers for the defendants, no strategy sessions with Schaden. He bided his time, monitoring the progress of other cases stemming from United 232, especially one case in Chicago that sought to establish liability, but not actual monetary damages, through a jury trial.

In Schaden's capable hands, our legal action moved at its own pace, which was slower than I'd originally hoped. It wasn't so much any great urgency to reap financial compensation that bothered me as it was the annoying notion that there were still loose ends lingering out there from flight 232, and I could do nothing to tie them up.

There was one point when I found myself between jobs and counting pennies to make sure we could make the rent, when I did break down and call Schaden to ask if there were something we could do to reach an agreement quickly. It was frightening, being suddenly unemployed and unsure how we would get by on just Diane's paycheck, and an infusion of cash seemed the simplest, easiest way to end the discomfort. Throughout the whole legal ordeal, from the moment I first decided to file an action, this was the only time the money seemed to matter, and it wasn't a question of want so much as need, or at least what seemed at the time to border on dire financial straits.

Part of the decision to ask about a settlement probably stemmed from my psychological and emotional condition, which was characterized by depression and self-doubt heightened by the simple absence of gainful employment. Diane had always been supportive whenever my career came to a fork in the road, but I had to admit to some minor pangs of male chauvinism when that support took the form of our only significant income. Family finances became tangled with my ego and, more significantly, with the persistent depression that was part of surviving the crash of United 232.

Schaden seemed to understand my position. It probably wasn't the first time he'd had to talk sense into an over-anxious client. But he maintained the big-picture philosophy that we'd adopted from the start, and politely explained that the timing wasn't right and that he could not advise a hasty settlement offer. His words made sense that slowly penetrated my fog of uncertainty. I trusted him completely and, sure enough, my sense of panic over our personal financial state eventually did subside. Diane pulled us both through, with her paycheck, unselfish love and understanding. Week by week we managed, and eventually I found another job to ease the strain — at least as far as money was concerned. Naturally, it wasn't long after I'd started drawing a salary again that the telephone rang and it was Dick Schaden.

"The timing is right," he said. "Here's what they'll do."

He gave me a number.

"I can push them," he offered.

"Take it," I said.

The first thing that occurred to me when I hung up the phone was that hiring Dick Schaden, instead of acting as my own counsel, was one of the luckiest things I'd done since I'd walked away from the burning airplane. With consummate professionalism that I could appreciate all the more after the succession of sleazy propositions lobbed my way, Schaden had negotiated a settlement everyone deemed fair — and one that was double what I'd originally asked for, which in turn was twice what the insurance agent had originally offered.

The second thing I thought of was all the bills I could pay off. The idea of finally being debt-free, even retiring the loan that had put me through law school, seemed like an unimaginable luxury.

People asked me where we were going with the money, as if everyone expected that we'd vacation in the South Pacific and sip umbrella drinks on the beach for the next six months. But the only time those thoughts entered our minds was when people asked. We'd never been much on extravagance, largely because it was beyond our means. But even this windfall, gained at a

119

price I still didn't understand, would be destined for the more mundane purpose of returning the family ledger to an even keel. There were no new cars or giant-screen TVs in our future.

I drove to Schaden's office in Boulder to pick up the check when it arrived. Dick wasn't in, but his assistant handed me the envelope with a smile.

"What are you going to spend it on?" she asked.

"Pay bills," I said.

Throughout the two years that it took to settle, I believe that at least subconsciously I felt that when the check finally came through there would be a few moments of elation, a sensation of well-being or at least the passing notion that it was kind of fun to be handed a large sum of money I never anticipated. But the only operative emotion for me at the time was relief, a thankfulness that this portion of the ordeal was over and done. I headed south on the Boulder Turnpike back toward Denver with an emptiness in the pit of my stomach where I thought I would feel satisfaction.

As the highway merged into Interstate 25, just north of the city, I thought about the money and was struck by a different sort of accounting, one that had nothing to do with bills and savings and student loans. Jay Ramsdell was still dead, Sylvia Tsao's little boy was still dead, and the only time I could see them alive anymore was in my nightmares.

The skyscrapers of downtown Denver loomed ahead on the interstate as my car completed the long, sloping right turn off the turnpike and sped closer to home, where I knew Diane would be no more excited than I was about this sudden change in our financial fortunes. The insurance check, the big, fat payoff for pain and suffering, sat on the seat next to me.

"Nothing's changed," I thought to myself.

Chapter

8

FOREVER CHANGED

It took many months to awaken to, much less acknowledge, the damage that the crash had inflicted on me. My mind and body would drop hints, some of them as subtle as a nagging pain in my neck and shoulders, some as heavy-handed as dreams that would reveal crash-related metaphors so obvious they could've found their way into a textbook for Psychology 101.

All these things I accepted as inevitable repercussions from my experience, and, individually, most of them could be dealt with. But I remained ignorant of their collective weight, even as the burden grew to almost crushing proportions. It was not so bad at first, in the days and weeks immediately after the crash, because I expected emotional vibrations. Some of these I even welcomed.

When two members of the CBA office staff, Colleen Miller and Christy Jordan, asked about setting up a memorial service for Jay Ramsdell, I thought it was a wonderful idea, even though I knew that I wasn't up to having any large role in its planning. So they made all the arrangements, reserving space at Flagstaff Amphitheater, a beautiful mountain park above Boulder, and making sure Jay's closest friends and colleagues were invited. My main contribution would be to say a few words about Jay and the childlike innocence he'd managed to maintain throughout his meteoric professional career. Although I certainly didn't plan to say much more, I wound up sharing a dream I had the night before the memorial, a vivid mini-drama that seemed appropriate under the circumstances.

Jay and I were sitting in a classroom, tucked behind desks, listening to a teacher lecture us about the plane crash that was to take place the next day. The teacher spoke calmly, matter-of-factly, about the circumstances that would unfold, about the people who would die, and we listened without horror or rage, simply accepting the inevitability of this pronouncement. Although the plane's fate was sealed, there seemed to be some room for compromise regarding what would happen to those aboard. The teacher explained that a certain number of lives would be taken, but tradeoffs were open to negotiation. For instance, he said, he would spare a baby but only if some other soul volunteered to take its place. From the corner of my eye I watched Jay's hand shoot instantly into the air, while the rest of the classroom sat there considering the offer.

In my heart, I knew the baby in question was Sabrina Michaelson, who I would find virtually unharmed in the wreckage. But while the dream scenario on its face seemed to illustrate a selfless quality we'd all come to recognize in Jay, and therefore became something positive and worth sharing at the memorial service, it also broached some larger questions whose impact I would feel welling inside me over the ensuing years. It hinted at tradeoffs with God. It reduced the tragedy to a strange game of musical chairs. And, most of all, it left me wondering why my hand didn't shoot up before Jay's. It left me asking why I'd sat there and let my best friend sacrifice himself while I merely entertained the option. It put my gathering guilt into a spiritual context that I wasn't equipped to confront.

There had been other troubling emotions, moments when I struggled to figure out my feelings and give them some sort of logical foundation. The first of these came on the first Sunday after the crash. Diane and I spent part of the morning crying through church and an emotional afternoon at Christy Jordan's mother's house, where we learned that Jay Ramsdell had officially been listed among the dead. We felt drained by the time we fell into bed, yet while Diane eventually drifted off to sleep I could not make my brain settle down. When the clock-radio showed midnight, I quietly got up and went downstairs to the living room of our town home and sat on the sofa. It seemed that there was something lodged between my subconscious and my waking thoughts that made sleep impossible, and I resolved to figure out what it was.

Just as I had sat in the National Guard building immediately after the crash and tried to retrace the events leading up to it, I sat in the darkness of my own home and replayed everything I could remember from the time the plane stopped skidding off the runway and through the cornfield. Straining to remember something I knew part of me had been trying to forget, I quickly saw an image jump into my mind's eye. It was vivid and clear and suddenly frozen in time. It was familiar and it was frightening. It was Sylvia Tsao, begging me to help her find her son.

My response, of course, had been to practically force her out of the burning wreckage by promising to find her little boy. The tiniest details of this brief encounter became huge to me. I had not said that I would try to look for the child. I hadn't said I would give it a shot, that I would look around before I left. I had told her that I would find her son. And the truth of the matter was that under the circumstances I could barely even make the attempt.

I stood up from the couch and headed to the kitchen. Earlier that day I had clipped an article from the newspaper that contained an updated status list of United 232's passengers. I found the clipping and switched on the light. Scanning the small type with bleary eyes, I zeroed in on one line of type that would haunt me for so very long to come.

Sylvia Tsao, alive. Infant son, missing.

I turned out the kitchen light and retreated to the darkness of the living room. I tried to rationalize. The airplane was rapidly filling with smoke. Flames shot at survivors as we made our way to the sunlit opening in the fuselage. An hysterical woman refused to leave an airplane that, I fully believed, would either burn up or explode in a matter of minutes, if not seconds. My immediate goal, my self-imposed responsibility, was to get her out of the airplane as quickly as possible. The only method at my disposal, or at least the only one that occurred to me under the stress of the moment, happened to be a promise I could not keep.

Maybe my strategy had actually saved the life of a woman who otherwise might have recklessly stumbled through the smoke searching for a child whose chances of survival did not, at that time, seem good. These were good, solid rationalizations. But they evaporated with the memory of those three words in the newspaper: *Infant son, missing.*

I had just spent four torturous days wondering about the fate of my best friend and I could not help but think about Sylvia Tsao. I could not help but think about what she must be going through, trying to cling to hope for the child who surely must have been the joy of her life. How much more does it hurt, I wondered, when the uncertainty involves your own flesh and blood? I felt tears again and then felt my lips moving silently in prayer for the woman and her little boy. I prayed again and again, clinging to the notion, cultivated by my Catholic upbringing, of power in repetition.

Two days later, I found an updated passenger status list — *Infant son, deceased.* My hope for Sylvia Tsao was gone, but my prayers never left her.

Six days after the crash, two days after receiving confirmation that Jay had died and the morning after a trip to the doctor had confirmed smoke inhalation, I walked back into the CBA office with the intention of resuming my job. Maybe it was part of my effort to rediscover routine or inject some fleeting sense of normalcy into my life and maybe it was, as I told myself at the time, that there was still work to be done and time would not stand still.

Some other survivors took extended time off from their jobs, which was understandable and maybe even the smartest thing to do, but my hard-headed insistence that I could handle things coaxed me to my office at 7 a.m. on Tuesday morning. Of course, I was not alone. Although there had been no staff meeting called to rally the troops and prop up morale, everyone understood that even under these terribly adverse conditions the daily operations of our business had to continue. Nobody called in to say they were taking a week off. Nobody broke down and said they just couldn't deal with the situation. No way could I sit home feeling sorry for myself while the rest of the office plodded on through a difficult time.

There were 74 pink telephone message slips waiting on my desk when I arrived that Tuesday following the crash. I know the number because I counted them. I told Susie Malin that I'd really need some help getting back to all these people, and with her assistance every call was indeed returned.

Some of the calls were from people whose names I recognized and some were from strangers, like the man who told me he had put a contract in the mail with the intention of securing rights to a movie about my role in the aftermath of the crash. I never got the contract and never heard from the man again (none of which meant that I wouldn't one day find my story, or at least portions of it, playing at the local movie theater).

Some of the messages were from blatant opportunists, some from respectable media outlets and some from what seemed like a combination of the two. I returned one call from a producer for the immensely popular Chicago-based TV talk show "Oprah!" and learned that they wanted me to fly there to be a guest. I didn't have any particular objection to appearing on the show, but it was also a simple fact that I didn't have time to spend an entire day on the road when there was work to be done at the CBA office. This news did not sit well with the producer, who then pressed me with the revelation that the Michaelsons already had agreed to be on. I told her I'd be happy to be on the show if I could do it from the studio of the show's Denver affiliate, via satellite hookup. When she told me that wouldn't do, I responded, as politely as I could, that it just wouldn't work out for me.

"You understand," said the producer impatiently, "that this is the Oprah Winfrey show, don't you?"

I said I did. Then she tried again to play me against Sabrina and her family.

"The Michaelsons are willing, so why aren't you?"

I had to laugh. And I did, literally, into the phone. It's some kind of brutal business when a producer tries to intimidate the survivor of an airline crash to hop on another plane to appear on her show. But my answer was still no. It was nothing against television. I would wind up appearing on other shows when time permitted, but this producer couldn't grasp the idea that, six days after the crash when I was trying to regain my bearings on the job, I didn't leap at the chance.

"You have an obligation — to your fellow survivors and to the families of those who died — to do the show," she insisted, finally pushing me too far.

"And I have an obligation," I replied evenly, "to hang up on you." And I did.

Many of the messages were from associates around the league calling to offer condolences for Jay's death and to ask how I was doing. One of the familiar names was that of a former CBA coach, and I dialed his number anticipating the same polite expressions of sympathy and concern. What I got was a rude wake-up call, my first indication that much of the professional world would return to business as usual long before I would be emotionally prepared to do so.

"How you doin', Jerry?" the coach asked.

"I'm hanging in there," I replied.

"Listen. I'll get right to the point. Jay promised me he would help me get the Santa Barbara coaching job. Now that he's gone and since you're probably gonna take over for him for awhile, I assume you're gonna help me get that job. I'm sure you agree with Jay that they have to have an experienced guy to coach in Santa Barbara . . ."

His voice held no compassion, no respect. It was just unvarnished self-interest that would not be affected by the simple fact that an airplane had fallen out of the sky and killed the man who might have helped him find work again as a basketball coach. Maybe I should have felt anger, but instead I felt sadness that a human being could act this coldly under these circumstances.

"I'm going to hang up the phone," I said, "and when I do, I'm going to try to forget that we ever had this conversation."

But I couldn't forget. The coach phoned probably ten times over the next few weeks and I never took his call. And I made sure somebody else got the Santa Barbara job.

The memorial service for Jay's CBA family happened later that same week, and the team owners who'd flown in for it remained in town to take care of some league business at a hotel near the airport. One of the items on the agenda was naming an interim commissioner. As Jay's deputy and one who'd worked closely with him on the all-important player and referee development contract with the NBA, I was the likely choice, and I'd already decided that if the appointment were offered, I would accept it.

In a conference room at the hotel, I conducted the meeting and, when the agenda arrived at the issue of an interim commissioner, I heard a motion that included my name, a second, and a unanimous voice vote of approval. The whole thing took perhaps 30 seconds and left me unexpectedly underwhelmed.

Although from the start I felt awkward about inheriting the job from my best friend who'd died in the same tragedy that had spared my own life, several people around the league filled my ear with talk about what a great opportunity this was, a real career-enhancer that could very well become a permanent appointment. Their words made some sense on an intellectual level, but did not sit right in my gut.

On the drive home from the owners' meeting, apprehension replaced the anticipation I might have felt had the job become mine under other circumstances. Within hours I felt genuine regret and the uneasiness that comes from committing to a wrong course of action. I'd made a mistake and I knew it, yet I also felt compelled to play the cards as they'd been dealt. I'd accepted the appointment as interim commissioner, and it didn't seem right to telephone the owners the next morning to say I really wasn't interested. On paper, the job looked terrific — even if it would involve twice the work and twice the commitment as my deputy commissioner's role.

Those were pivotal times for the CBA, and I must admit they were exciting times, but they were also demanding times. To do the job well would require equal parts competence and passion, the precise mix of qualities that Jay had brought to the table. If I had reservations about any one aspect of the position, it was the necessity of doing business effectively with 16 very different owners, some with incredible egos. The rest of the job, and particularly the negotiations on a new NBA contract, didn't seem so daunting. I was excited about the challenge of negotiating that deal, especially after meeting NBA commissioner David Stern and his deputy commissioner, Russ Granik. I liked both men personally and even though I knew they were tough negotiators, I also knew they would be fair.

I had enough faith in my abilities to competently handle the work of commissioner of the CBA, but I would have been lying to myself to think I could step into Jay's shoes the way I did and feel much zest for the work ahead. At the time, I think I accurately foresaw the enormity of the challenge for the league and whoever sat in the commissioner's chair. What I underestimated was the slow, unrelenting psychological impact the crash of United 232 would have on my own life. I worked hard to establish myself in the commissioner's role, but it was never a comfortable fit, and before long I let it be known that I didn't want the job on a permanent basis.

It wasn't so much the tangible elements of the work as just a lingering unhappiness. There was an unshakable notion that this was not the way things were meant to be. A trained counselor might have been able to track my emotional state and explain exactly why this had happened, but counseling was for other folks, those unfortunate people who had real problems. So I thought.

About five months later, on January 4, 1990, the CBA announced that Irv Kaze, a former media relations director for both the New York Yankees and Los Angeles Raiders, would take over as the league's new commissioner. I went back to my previous duties as deputy commissioner and resolved to give it a chance, to see if I could find the same level of personal and professional chemistry with Irv that Jay and I had shared. But it became harder and harder to perform the simple physical act of going to work every day, much less do the job. By February, I knew that the situation just wasn't going to work, and the only real decision that remained was when and how to exit as gracefully as possible.

I wrote a letter to Irv explaining my desire to leave the CBA and put it on his desk as I was about to leave the office for an out-of-town trip. My hope was that he'd read the letter while I was gone and I wouldn't have to deal with the repercussions immediately, but Irv caught me almost literally heading out the door and we settled the matter then and there. He asked only that I stay on during a transitional period and I agreed. It was a relief to have the situation resolved, and I officially resigned in April, whereupon the stress of being stuck in the wrong job was replaced by the stress of having no job at all.

The symptoms of my declining days with the CBA would have given any trained counselor a road-map to my psychological diagnosis. My demeanor around the office probably reflected all the textbook signs of post-traumatic stress disorder, on which all of us who survived United 232 had been briefed immediately after the crash. Of course, I couldn't see the forest for the trees.

Anger and guilt came and went, while physical energy deteriorated until I assumed a near zombie-like state. Sleeplessness dogged me and, on those rare occasions when I did slip into slumber, nightmares followed. There remained only two constants in my emotional life — depression, which I refused to recognize in its clinical form, and Diane, who had no more idea how to deal with these symptoms than I did. The difference was that she, at least, made an effort.

Diane would propose that we do things to help me out of the doldrums — a movie, dinner, anything — but I would usually decline. She would suggest a vacation and I would find an excuse not to go. She knew that exercise usually helped clear my mind and so she would encourage me go for long-distance runs. But I seldom found the energy to do even that.

Diane never pushed me hard, she simply let her suggestions float in the air until I'd shot them down and then we would move on to another topic. Being around me, I'm sure, was like walking on eggshells for her, an experience frightening for her on two levels. She saw me slipping into some dark world and feared losing the man she'd married, yet she avoided pressing the issue for fear of making things worse. The worst part about what was happening to me was seeing its effects in her eyes and knowing that I had already pushed her love and patience beyond any reasonable human limits. Although still in a prolonged period of denial, I was not totally blind to the effects of my emotional upheaval. While on the one hand I tried to make myself ignore it, on the other I simply felt powerless to reverse it.

When I made the decision to quit the CBA, hinting that I might again pursue my original dream of sportscasting, Diane gritted her teeth and put on the brave face once again. She told me to go for it. She told me not to worry about how we'd get by while I looked for an opening, that we'd find a way to make it work. She had stood by me once already when I'd made a run at becoming an NBA broadcaster, but that was when I'd been behaving like a reasonably normal person. Now she was making the same sacrifice for a man wrestling with forces he could not even see or name, a man who had simply stopped living a portion of his life. She was still standing by a man who, it must have seemed, was slipping farther away from her by the day and did not have the good sense to seek help.

My love for Diane never changed, but the everyday ways that I tried to nurture our marriage fell victim to the same indifference that ultimately moved me to quit my job. Knowing that I wasn't being a good husband was one thing, and finding the will to do something about it was a completely different story. I was a walking case study of fully-conscious, emotional paralysis.

I figured that time was on my side and eventually I would win the battle with my psychological enemies. I figured that I could handle things on my own. And then I figured, as I sat unemployed, that I should just snap open a few beers in the early evening until I felt a little different, a little deadened to the pain.

When Gary Priest, another survivor who'd become a good friend, suggested a gathering of United 232 alumni, I jumped at the chance. These weren't so much therapy sessions in the technical sense as social gatherings fueled by the intense need — I felt it and I'm sure some others did, too — to be with people who'd experienced the same life-changing event. The magnetic pull of this common bond was hard to explain and probably in some ways threatening to survivors' family members who hadn't been on the plane, but it was very real. The movie <u>Fearless</u> explored the phenomenon quite vividly in depicting Jeff Bridges' character, Max Klein, cultivating relationships with both the boy he had comforted on the airplane and a woman who'd lost her infant son in the crash. That kinship with other survivors actually put distance between Klein and his family. Nothing so dramatic happened to me — notwithstanding my movie-going friends' misplaced assumption that I'd actually had an affair with another survivor — but there always was that feeling of connection to others in the tragedy that threatened normal family dynamics.

For about a month after I left my job with the CBA, the desire to down a few beers in the middle of the afternoon became more intense and had begun to represent a red flag, a sign of trouble that even I could not totally ignore. And so I made an appointment with a trauma counselor, someone Gary Priest had recommended. This was not exactly the first counselor I'd seen, as the airline had arranged for someone to give us a general idea of what to expect, psychologically speaking, shortly after the crash. The CBA office also had called in a counselor to speak to the staff regarding the loss of Jay and I had gone a couple of times with Jay's girlfriend, Lori Overstreet, when she had appointments with her counselor — although in that case I saw my role as moral support, not prospective client.

Friends had suggested that I see somebody and the thought even came to me all by itself a few times when I'd hit an emotional downward spiral. But I never seriously entertained the notion of seeking professional help until I found myself staring into the refrigerator again and again on weekday afternoons, looking for an answer. Finally, I made an appointment.

Exactly what I expected from the counselor, I'm not sure. Maybe a sympathetic ear, a verbal pat on the back and reassurances that, with time, everything would return to normal. We chatted for about 30 minutes and I filled her in on the emotional ride that had sapped me of my energy, my drive and my natural instinct to care about the things most important to me. Then she spoke four words that scared me to death.

"You're suffering from depression."

At first, I couldn't believe I was hearing them, but slowly they sank in, leaving me speechless. I buried my face in my hands, feeling both disbelief and shame build into full-fledged nausea.

The counselor began talking again. I could hear her voice, but the words were just sounds that passed in one ear and out the other. The only word that echoed in my head was *depression*.

I tried to process this diagnosis and met resistance at every turn. Depression wasn't something that happened to people like me, people who considered themselves reasonably well-adjusted. Depression only afflicted people who weren't quite tough enough to handle what life threw at them. People who'd been seriously abused. People who'd experienced a whole laundry list of personal loss — not somebody who'd been delivered by fate from what appeared to be certain death. And so I arrived at the conclusion that the counselor was simply wrong, that she had known me for exactly 30 minutes whereas I had known myself for 30 years.

She continued to talk and I continued to pretend to listen, quite possibly missing something of value she had to say but unable to focus on anything except the idea that I had been diagnosed as suffering from clinical depression. Slowly, though, the certainty that she was wrong began to fade as I took inventory of the things I'd been feeling for the last several months.

It was a brutal checklist: I didn't give a damn about anything in my professional life. My marriage, which I had watched erode to the point that my wife must have felt she was living with a stranger, didn't seem to matter. Other members of my immediate family, who'd been so supportive of me, hardly merited a second thought in my self-absorbed state of mind. There was no way I could face these realities and cling to the notion that nothing was wrong that a little time wouldn't fix. I found myself moving from complete denial to a willingness to entertain the idea that the diagnosis might be right.

Suddenly, I realized that the room had gone silent. The counselor had stopped talking and sat there looking at me, waiting for a response. I'm not sure where the words came from, but I spoke.

"Tell me about depression," I said. "About the depression I have."

"What you're experiencing is very, very common for someone like you who has been in a plane crash," she explained. "It's a very natural consequence. Its also a very mild depression. I've seen about 15 survivors now from your crash and I think you might actually be doing better than *all* of them. Your having depression doesn't mean you're crazy. It means you're normal."

That explanation sounded incredibly reassuring, and the competitive athlete in me found some strange comfort in the fact that the counselor felt I was probably doing better than the rest of her clients from United 232, as if our comparative psychological conditions were being judged on points. The utter normalcy of my condition cheered me, and before long I wrapped myself in a comforting rationalization — "I'm only human" — and admitted my frailties to myself. But there would be one other shock before I left.

At the end of the session she suggested that I might want to go on Prozac, as some other crash survivors had, to even out my emotional ride. She never actually recommended it, but just hearing her invoke the name of the drug made me nervous. While practicing law in Kansas, I had represented several clients in mental illness hearings, where my clients' families or the state proposed to commit them to a mental institution. Many of those clients were on Prozac, and they all had serious problems. While I might have been ready to face the reality of my depression, I certainly wasn't prepared to surrender my head to prescription medication.

I immediately dismissed the Prozac idea and eventually left the counselor's office feeling better than I had in weeks. At home that night I enjoyed the first truly restful night's sleep in months and felt like I'd started to kick the psychological funk that had cast a shadow over me and everyone whose life had touched mine in the last nine months. I felt almost euphoric, buoyed by the feeling that my life seemed on the road to recovery — until I woke up the next morning.

Diane had already left for work, which meant that I was home alone, which in turn reminded me that I was unemployed and had no immediate professional prospects. The guilt and anger over the crash that came and went now were joined by guilt and anger over my job situation, or lack of one. I felt a gathering sense of panic, a need to regain control.

I sat down in a lawn chair on the small deck outside our town home, staring at the front range of the Rocky Mountains that stretched to the north and south as far as the eye could see. Our dog, Shoshone, curled up at my feet. The mountains often have a calming effect on people, and the way they rose into the blue sky that late spring day, snow-caps brushing against the clouds, made my vantage point well-suited to reflection and contemplation.

I tried to clear my head and get back to the point of emotional equilibrium that I'd felt less than 24 hours earlier, in the counselor's office.

My method was simple: I would assess the problem, settle on a course of action and then execute it. Although I'd been trying to do that for months without much success, it seemed that now I possessed the critical tool I'd been lacking. I'd come to grips with the idea that I was depressed, in the clinical sense as well as the obvious one, and that acceptance surely would help me over the hump. Or so I thought.

My mind churned everything over and over. I analyzed my guilt, assessed my anger and mentally charted the downward path on which depression had taken me and those closest to me. But instead of visualizing a solution, I found myself staring into a black void. It didn't matter how my circumstances were arranged or rearranged. It didn't matter how many times I disassembled and reconstructed my brief but haunting encounter with Sylvia Tsao. It didn't matter what rationalization I chose to frame the loss of my colleague and best friend Jay Ramsdell. The pit was too deep to climb out of, even with the counselor's comforting words still ringing in my ears.

The morning hours slipped by without any change in my condition, and when I looked at my watch and saw it was noon already, I climbed out of my chair on the deck and went inside to fix some lunch. It was a reflex move, one last thread of normalcy to which I could cling, but I simply wasn't hungry. Appetites of all sorts had almost disappeared. I couldn't even motivate myself to fix a sandwich.

With a wave of self-pity threatening to send me under, I summoned one last shred of emotional energy and determined that I would tackle the effects of the crash head-on. In the garage I rooted around and found the large box of newspaper and magazine clippings that Diane and I had saved over the previous nine months. I brought the box into the living room and set it on the coffee table. This seemed like the only way I could still confront what had happened to me, by rummaging through the media coverage and reliving as much of the ordeal as I could.

It didn't take long for the tears to come, but for the most part, this exercise felt like treading water. I neither sank nor swam.

Red-eyed and surrounded by scraps of paper that whispered memories in my ear, it occurred to me that perhaps this was simply one of those days, a bump in the road on the way to somewhere better, an inevitable false step on the way to recovery. The quicker I could get through the day, I thought, the better off I'd be. Slowly, a plan developed: I would go to a bar just a few blocks from home and just start drinking.

A glance at my watch and some quick calculation revealed a three-hour window of opportunity before Diane would get home from work. I could get comfortably numb, return before my wife arrived and simply go to sleep, effectively killing the rest of the day by putting it, and myself, out of our misery. It might not have been a great plan, it might have been clinically flawed, but it was a plan nonetheless and I decided to go with it. First, though, I would clean up the mess of news clippings that I'd spread over the coffee table and living room floor.

As I grabbed piles of newsprint and stuffed them back into the box, my eyes fell on a photograph. It was a picture of Diane and me, hugging each other in the lobby of the CBA office. It had been taken by a photographer who had claimed to be from the London Times, but we'd found his work on the pages of Star magazine, the supermarket tabloid, next to a typically sensational story about me and Sabrina Michaelson, the "miracle child." The story might have been a bit overdone, but the photograph spoke pure, undiluted truth. When we'd first seen the picture, we'd thought it was a nice shot. But now it literally moved me to tears.

The picture reminded me how much I loved her, how strong and steadfast she'd been, even as I seemed to push her away and become increasingly self-absorbed. It reminded me of how she had sacrificed so much in her life for me.

Already in the nine short months since the crash I'd heard about an alarming number of couples connected to United 232 who'd been unable to reconnect and had watched their relationship slide irretrievably into divorce. I knew it could happen to Diane and me. Maybe it was already happening, but neither of us had quite been able to put words to this slow, quiet tragedy.

All of this hit home in a matter of seconds, as the photo of our embrace grabbed me and shook me, like a friend trying to shake some sense into a fool. I forgot about going to the bar and settled on what I knew was a much healthier form of therapy. Slipping on some running shoes, I headed out for a long run. It was one last attempt to clear my head and achieve some helpful perspective on my life.

I must have run several miles, certainly longer than the mile or two I was normally limited to because of the pain in my back. And for that slice of time my mind seemed separate from my body except for the runner's high that swept over me after a short time. When I finally returned home, I felt good. Not only had the physical rhythms of my own breathing and the sound of my footsteps fostered a sense of well-being, but there was a lingering sense of accomplishment that I'd rarely felt since leaving my job. I had done the right thing, dismissing the desire to drown my sorrows. But the euphoria was short-lived, and didn't even last until I got out of the shower. There was hardly space in the bathroom for all the demons that came back to visit me.

Guilt, anger, injured pride over my unemployment, uncertainty about the future, a growing sense of meaninglessness about life — they all crowded around me until the despair I'd felt before my run had returned, intensified, and hung around my neck like a great stone weight.

Whether it was the simple fatigue of the run or the crushing pressure of my depression or some combination of the two, I found myself slumping into a rocking chair in our bedroom. For what must have been the millionth time since the crash, I rewound the mental videotape of my life to a point about a year earlier and played it again, starting with our move from Topeka to Denver. That had been such an exciting time for Diane and me, full of promise, as I joined Jay in the CBA office and embarked on what surely appeared to be an upward climb, both personally and professionally. Three months later I was sitting in an airplane when something exploded, and the descent that took

45 minutes to hit the ground now had continued for 10 months. I shook my head in disbelief that my life had become this screwed up so quickly.

I had gone from successful sportscaster and sports administrator to mental patient.

Struggle as I might to regain control of my life, it had careened beyond my grasp, rendering me a clinical case with an illness that had a name easily mentioned in the same breath with the word Prozac. Now, I dissolved into tears without a second thought, and they wouldn't stop until I heard a door close downstairs and footsteps across the floor. Diane was home, and I thought for a second of leaving the chair to go and greet her, but my legs wouldn't move. I heard her climbing the stairs to our room and still I sat silent and motionless, waiting for the moment she would walk through the door and comfort me with her warmth and her words.

"I'm having a real tough time, honey," I said, as soon as she entered the room, stating what was not only obvious to her, but tiresome and familiar. It was my spoken solicitation of pity, the opening line of a dialogue we had rehearsed before. As if following the script, she knelt down beside my chair and put her arms around me. But then she veered off in a very different direction.

Her embrace was quick and she pulled back as if its purpose were merely to serve notice that her patience was not boundless, and that what she was about to say deserved my full attention. She waited until my eyes met hers squarely.

"I get my strength from God," she said, letting the words sink in. Then she stood up and left the room.

So drastically had Diane departed from our usual give-and-take that I found myself speechless, unable to offer any response before she slipped out the room and was gone. I was too startled to be angry, too stunned by what she said to even think about getting up.

It was as if she had thrown me some kind of lifeline, tossed it into the water as a last resort, the last thing she could think of that might help me. And I hesitated to grab it.

Anchored to the Midwestern ideal of stubborn self-sufficiency, I could not immediately bring myself to accept her words. She had always displayed strength of a quiet and confident kind, and it was never any secret that her spiritual faith was its foundation. But I don't think I'd ever heard her say it so directly, and with a tone that sounded more like a challenge than a simple statement of fact.

Over the previous months I had gradually backed her against a wall, draining her of compassion, and then she'd arrived home from work one night to find me almost despondent in the rocking chair, demanding more. She responded with perhaps all she had left.

"I get my strength from God."

The pure truth was undeniable, but I wanted to fight off her challenge. It seemed to demand an acknowledgment of defeat. Still, I listened to what Diane said, again and again in my head, until the voice became less and less hers and more and more my own. I had nothing left to throw at the problem and Diane had just flung me her own last, best hope. I closed my eyes and bowed my head.

"God, for the first time in my life I admit that I've been defeated," I prayed. "Please come into my life and help me because I can't do it on my own. Please just give me some kind of relief from this battle and this pain. Just come into my life. Help me. Please."

Physically, at that moment, I felt suddenly and inexplicably energized, like an overheated distance runner taking the first cold, clean swallows of water at the end of his run. Emotionally, I felt soothed by an amazing sense of calm, as if I'd just been injected with the knowledge that everything would eventually turn out all right.

It would be far from the truth to say that everything was, indeed, all right from that point on. I don't believe there is a magic pill that makes the kind of guilt I felt about Jay Ramsdell, Sylvia Tsao and her little boy and the other 109 people who perished in United 232 go away. There is little relief from losing a friend like Jay, and no sure-fire way to come to grips with the question, "Why me?" Depression does not disappear overnight. And though the nightmares came less frequently from that point on, they've never quite gone away.

But spiritually, that time in the semi-darkness of our bedroom when I reeled from the impact of Diane's simple pronouncement gave me a new starting point. It was like finding myself hopelessly lost and finally swallowing my pride long enough to stop and ask directions.

I'd fallen 36,000 feet in a DC-10 — and a lot farther in the shell of depression and self-pity — to finally touch God.

I was changed. Forever.

Chapter

9

BREAKFAST WITH THE CAPTAIN

On the sixth anniversary of United 232's crash landing, Al Haynes observed certain personal rites as he does every year on July 19. He lowered the flag at his home in Seattle to half-staff. He also took the day off from his beloved pastime umpiring local Little League games and he fielded a telephone call from Dr. Mike Sturgis, the psychiatrist who talked him through the days immediately after the incident.

Those rituals fulfilled, Haynes, who retired as a United captain after 35 years of service, returned in the following days to a self-imposed regimen of travel that finds him living out of a suitcase more than he ever did in his years with the airline and speaking far more passionately from the podium than he ever did from the cockpit, where pilots generally confine their speech to describing what you can see if you look out the left side of the aircraft.

Five days after his observance of the anniversary, he bounded down the stairs of a hotel across the street from Denver's now-defunct Stapleton International Airport, where United 232 had originated. He'd given a presentation the night before in the mountain town of Breckenridge to a convention of the Kansas Farmers Association and had been scheduled to fly out of Denver early that morning, but when I called and asked if we could get together, he immediately changed his departure to the afternoon and agreed to meet for breakfast.

We were not strangers. We'd spoken before on many occasions, at memorials and in support sessions shortly after the crash, and I'd heard the presentation he gives on the lecture circuit. Yet we'd never sat down and shared our thoughts in any depth, and I still had questions. Some, like those concerning the activity in the cockpit during the 45 minutes we passengers silently considered the merits and misgivings of lives that seemed about to end, he had addressed in press conferences that I'd watched on television and in articles that I'd read, but I still wanted to hear the answers all over again, in person, without the media's filters.

Those of us who survived the crash could not escape the single most troubling question: Why? We could ignore it for awhile, forestall the inevitable confrontation with the mystery of our survival, but eventually we would have to stare down fate and settle on a reason we were still here.

We explored different avenues in search of the answer — some spiritual, some practical, some psychological. It was the kind of question that invited introspection and contemplation yet also held the danger of pulling one deep into a philosophical maze that offered no clean way out, no satisfactory solution. At one point in the months following the crash, Haynes woke up in a hotel room somewhere on the lecture circuit and settled on a disarmingly simple answer: He lived to talk.

Al Haynes did not seem to struggle with the aftermath of the crash the way I had. The questions that gnawed at me, the issues that periodically paralyzed me, never kept the captain — the man whose intimacy with the dire details of a doomed flight could have haunted him endlessly — from moving ahead with his life. In all the nights since the crash, he never had a single nightmare, not a single subconscious replay. The night before we met for breakfast, perhaps anticipating our conversation, I dreamed I was once again aboard United 232, except this time my two-year-old daughter was with me — the child who hadn't even been conceived as I took inventory in the minutes before touch-down. How had Al Haynes managed to avoid the repercussions?

More than anything, I wondered if his carefully scripted talks were his release — a pilot's controlled, verbal navigation of a flight on which he felt technically powerless — repeated hundreds of times with therapeutic effect. Haynes admitted that indeed they were his therapy, but he took the notion a step further. When he confronted the big question about his survival, the mystery that launched others among us on philosophical or spiritual searches for our place in the grand scheme of things, he found the answer in this accidental avocation, these hour and a half oral presentations he has delivered so many times. It was an astoundingly simple revelation for him, and the only one that made sense.

"It is why I survived," he said, setting his fork on the plate and leaving it there. "That's my explanation for why I survived."

He pondered the big question again, for perhaps half a second, and elaborated.

"Why did I survive? I have absolutely no reason why I'm alive, so I use the talks as why, because I'll never really know. It's the question you can't answer. For instance, I read about one young man on the flight and he was told by one of the passengers that the best thing he could do would be to take his seat belt off prior to the crash and *not* be strapped in when the airplane hit the ground. And he did, and the airplane broke where he was sitting, so he was thrown out. I'm not sure, but I think the article said he was the only one in his row who survived. Talk about 'Why me?' "

Then Haynes told another story that had unfolded about a year earlier when a 14-year-old crash survivor, who'd been about 9 at the time of the incident, met with him before one of his talks. Haynes always makes a habit of meeting with any survivors who watch his presentation so he can tell them what he's going to talk about and what video aids he's going to use, and so they can leave the room if they think the experience might become too intense.

"And his mother was there," Haynes continued, "and we talked, something about swapping seats that some families did so they could be next to every child. And the boy said, 'Yeah, I swapped seats, at the very start of the trip. This lady traded seats with me.' I said, 'Do you know what happened to the lady?' He said, 'Yeah, she didn't survive.' And his mother said, 'What?' So for five years that kid had been living with the thought that had he not changed seats... and he never said a thing to his mother. Whether it affected him or not, I don't know. It sure looked like it when I asked him."

There was silence when Haynes finished telling the story, and I wondered whether the younger survivors on the flight had been cushioned by their youth. Or had they merely been granted a reprieve until some later time, years ahead? Would they find something to cling to like Al Haynes, who found reason enough for living in the motivational speeches that suddenly seemed such a perfect fit?

"I don't know why I started," he said. "I was asked to give this talk to a friend of mine's Kiwanis meeting. And then another friend of mine who's in our Little League, he has the Lions

Club or something, said he'd like for me to tell them what happened. From that, I ended up doing a Rotary Club, then Rotary International. There was something about the way it fell into place, with no advertising. I don't belong to a speaker's bureau or anything like that, and I get more of these than I can handle. The only reason I'm doing it is because that's why I'm here."

People simply asked and Al Haynes could not say no. By the sixth anniversary of the crash, he had averaged about 100 engagements a year, speaking to corporations, students, civic groups, military outfits — almost anyone who requested his presence and was willing to make a donation to one of four causes. Two of them are scholarship funds set up to honor people who died in the crash. Another is the Seattle Little League, an organization to which Haynes has devoted both his time and his heart. Since United Airlines, several years earlier, generously offered to pick up his airline travel costs for the talks, he asks only that his host provide him with lodging, meals and a lift to and from the airport.

The story of Haynes' and my survival — of anyone's survival really — isn't easily explained. Still, I hoped the captain could shed light on it, over breakfast. I needed to hear, firsthand, how he and first officer Bill Records, second officer Dudley Dvorak, off-duty captain Dennis Fitch and a host of other professionals in the air and on the ground had guided the hopelessly crippled DC-10 to the landing strip by the cornfield where tragedies and miracles unfolded.

"We were just over an hour out," Haynes began, sounding as if he were delivering this explanation for the first time when in fact he had lost count years ago. "We'd finished lunch. We were on a radar vector to get behind traffic and they'd just turned us back to the east. We heard a bang. I'm sitting with my coffee in my hand, Bill's at the throttle. Fortunately, we were in level flight.

"'What the hell is that?' I think that's what I said. It was a loud bang, a very loud bang. This brief vibration followed. We

147

had no idea what was going on. We did know we'd lost the number two engine. That was very easy, all the gauges read zero for the number two. It wasn't hard to figure out.

"We didn't know why that sucker blew like that. Then Bill said, 'I can't control the airplane.' We're in a pretty steep bank and the nose is going down. Yet he's got the controls just the opposite, which you can't do at that altitude. I looked around and said the dumbest thing I ever said in my life. I said, 'I got it, Bill.' That's what you say when one person's handing over controls to the other. But obviously, I didn't have it. We closed the throttle on the left side and pushed up the throttle on the right side. Why we did it, we have no idea, but that's what leveled the airplane."

Even those who knew next to nothing about the technical capabilities of airplanes, much less the complex workings of the DC-10, came to understand the basic elements of what had happened to us. Three hydraulic lines controlled the plane's steering. When the number two engine, the one situated just above the fuselage at the tail, exploded, all three lines were severed, virtually disabling conventional means of controlling our elevation and direction. The people who wrote the pilot's manual for the DC-10 regarded this sort of mid-air happening as impossible, because when Haynes and the others tore through the book looking for solutions they found none, except a page that dealt with loss of manual controls, but even that did not go into any significant detail.

When Haynes radioed United's System Aircraft Maintenance control center (SAM) and announced his dire situation, he got the impression that initially nobody there believed that the on-board diagnosis, triple hydraulic failure, actually could have happened.

At one point, a member of the cockpit crew who I later learned was Dvorak passed by my aisle seat on the way to the rear of the aircraft, presumably to try to check out the damage. On his way back to the cockpit, the plane pitched and he grabbed the back of my seat to steady himself. I remember looking at his face, focusing on his eyes for a split-second and hoping to see the precise seriousness of our situation reflected there. I saw no panic but felt only mildly reassured.

"So we fly fairly straight for awhile, then start another right turn, then a series of right turns," Haynes continued. "The airplane wants to turn right all the time because of the added drag on the right side of the airplane. We didn't think we could turn left, so we'd go 360 degrees and come back to where we wanted. But you know, somebody asked me, 'Why did you go to Sioux City?' I said we didn't. The airplane went to Sioux City."

In the cabin, we could hear the two wing engines alternately increase and decrease thrust as we almost rhythmically rose and fell through the air. Pilots call the technique "porpoising" and use it to maintain control under adverse conditions like those affecting us. We waited to hear definitive news from the cockpit about what lay in store, hoping to detect from the captain's voice the same sort of reading I'd sought in Dvorak's eyes.

In the years I'd traveled extensively on the airlines, it had become almost habit upon boarding a plane to glance into the cockpit for a glimpse of the captain. I assigned no deep meaning or significance to this exercise beyond the vague comfort that came from seeing a pilot who looked the part of the experienced veteran. The more gray hair, the better. It was simple enough to take a peek in smaller aircraft, where the entry door takes passengers right past the cockpit, but the DC-10 is configured differently and I'd not laid eyes on Al Haynes. This dawned on me the first time Haynes came on the intercom to announce that we had trouble. My only measure of the man, at that moment, was his voice. He sounded like an older pilot, experienced, confident and reassuring. I wouldn't know what he looked like until the news media picked up our story and flashed his picture everywhere.

Al Haynes had flown four years in the Marine Corps and joined the airline in 1956. Of his 35 years as a commercial pilot, he'd spent nine as a co-pilot on the DC-10, where he eventually accumulated almost 7,200 hours in the air — the better part of a whole year. But in the minutes leading up to the touch-down in Sioux City, it was the voice that I clung to, the voice that I balanced against the fear of impending disaster when Haynes spoke to us for the last time before impact.

"The cockpit voice recorder for some reason didn't pick up what I said and everybody has a different idea of what I said," he explained. "But I do know I started with 'I'm not going to kid you.' I know I started that way. I said something to the effect that the loss of the engine caused some damage to our ability to control the aircraft, and we're going to land in Sioux City, Iowa. And I said the landing will probably be very hard, harder than anything you've been through. One guy said in an interview right after the crash that I said everything would be OK. I don't believe I ever said that."

Of that I, too, was fairly certain. A promise of deliverance coming from the cockpit would have been impossible to forget. But fear, coupled with an intense desire for the ordeal to end safely and the firm, professional tone of Al Haynes' voice might have led some passengers to hear reassurance that simply wasn't there.

"My concern was what was going to happen after we landed," Haynes went on. "We could see the runway. We thought we could land the airplane, but we had no control of the airplane once we landed. We can't steer to keep it on the runway. The absolute best thing I can see happening to us is staying on the runway somehow and going off the end of the runway and stopping in the mud. Worst-case scenario for me was hitting the runway and going off to the side and maybe hitting a fire truck, shearing the gear and ripping the engines off. But those things I didn't have time to think about."

Of course, those of us in the cabin had plenty of time to think. From 3:16 p.m., when the engine blew, to 4:00 p.m., when lives ended or changed forever, we confronted our mortality. Afterward, Haynes would think long and hard about the time that had sped by so fast. He looked down into what remained of his breakfast for a long moment.

"It had to be hell for the passengers," he finally said. "I really felt sorry for them. That's the worst part about being a passenger. You have no control. That's why a lot of people don't like to fly. For us up front, though, it was like this: You're driving down the road and a ball rolls in front of the car. You swerve to miss the ball, and you slip off on the shoulder of the road and kind of fight to get control of the car back. You get about six blocks down the road and your legs start to shake and you break out in a sweat. But while you're doing it, you don't have time to think about it. Our 'swerve' took 45 minutes. Just as soon as we'd do one thing, we'd have to do something else. We were constantly looking for an answer, so it was the shortest 45 minutes of my life. But it had to be the longest 45 minutes for the passengers, because they didn't know what was going on. It's not that we wanted to keep them in the dark. But we didn't know for sure where we were going. I'd heard that some relatives of the dead said, 'Well, if he had known what was going on, maybe my husband could have written a letter.' I understand some people did, but it probably wouldn't have survived the crash. Did you think about that, Jerry?"

I explained that one rather mundane order of business had suddenly acquired a sense of urgency: I'd bought a life insurance policy some weeks earlier and had forgotten to tell Diane about it. Convinced at that moment on the DC-10 that I wasn't going to make it, I wrote a note explaining where I'd left the policy and then slipped the paper into my briefcase, figuring it stood a better chance of survival than me. Haynes listened with interest and then asked if, after the crash, I'd ever recovered my briefcase. I shook my head.

"I don't know if this is a true story or not," he said, "but I heard that after the crash there was one survivor walking around

151

the wreckage and he saw his briefcase lying on the runway. So he walked over to get it and just as he got there a fire truck ran over it."

We both laughed, in the way people who have been immersed in a common tragedy find release in such dark humor. Haynes, whose compassion for the crash victims and accessibility to survivors ultimately lent depth and texture to our first sketchy outline of him, surprised me with his mostly self-deprecating wit. It had surfaced even as he lay only semi-conscious at the crash scene, his 10-foot high cockpit compressed to less than a third of that space until it looked like nothing but a cocoon of wires. Haynes didn't know where in the world he was, dead or alive. His last vivid memories were of the approach and touchdown.

"We asked the tower if there was anything flat out there, if there was a place we could put down, something closer than Sioux City," he said. "That's when they thought about the freeway. That's why they went out and cleared all the exits to the freeway so there'd be no cars out there. But I'd never put it on a freeway. I'd put it on a field next to a freeway, but you can't put an airplane that size down on a freeway, there's too many light standards and signs that could rip fuel tanks open.

"We got the idea there were only certain things we could do. We'd say, 'left, right, forward' and 'back,' call it out. If that right wing started down, the first one who saw it would yell, 'Left!' As we're getting close to the ground, we're pretty well lined up with the runway, but the right wing starts down. So Bill's saying "Left, left, left" to get the right wing up. We're going about 245 miles an hour. We're really scooting across the ground. Normal is 120 knots, or about 140 miles an hour. We hit the ground and I thought we'd landed. Of course, I got knocked out immediately. I remember nothing at all of the crash. I do remember the impact. To me it was like if you're folding up an air mattress, finally getting all the air out, that last big push goes whoosh. I don't remember a bang or thud, but a whoosh. That's the sound I recall. Dudley said I talked right after we stopped. I know that tremendous pressure was on my back. He said he talked to me and I said, 'Where are you?' And he said, 'I'm on top of you.' And I said, 'You've got to lose some weight, you're pretty heavy.'

"I did wake up, and there was not a sound. I mean not a sound. It's a poor choice of words, but it was deathly quiet. No sirens, couldn't see anything, hear anything. The first thing that came to my mind was an out-of-body experience. I kept thinking there had to be some kind of noise. I thought we'd landed the airplane. But there was no flash of light, no reliving life, nothing in slow motion. Then I passed out again. They told me it was about 30 minutes after the crash when they found us. I remember the pressure coming off my back. What a relief that was. I remember being pulled out of the plane on my stomach, asking, 'Did everybody make it?' Somebody said no. My response was — and I do remember this — 'I killed people.' Somebody said, 'No you didn't, you saved people.' I guess it depends on how you look at it. That's why I was a little concerned about the support group meetings, where other people there might say I killed their daughter or son. And I wouldn't blame them. But I never heard that. Ever.

"I don't remember the ride to town or getting out of the ambulance. I remember coming to, in the emergency room, being on my stomach and seeing all these legs. I remember the sound of cutting my clothes off. I told them if the front of my pants is wet, that's coffee. They said yeah, sure, they'd heard that before.

My mother would've been very, very proud of me. That day, in Denver, I'd unwrapped a brand new pair of underwear. They're cutting off these dark, dark clothes and as they peel back my pants I've got on this pair of Jockey briefs, the brief briefs, white with green stripes. The nun and chaplain are there and the nun said to her, 'Look at those cute white bikinis.' I don't remember that, but they told me.

"Next thing I remember is waking up, in the room, and the surgeon is there, cleaning out my scalp. He was apologizing for the pain because he couldn't give me a general anesthetic because of the concussion. I didn't feel a thing. As he sewed me up, he'd have to stick me with an injection again and again. Nothing. A second plastic surgeon came in, and I asked him to take a couple of tucks while he was at it."

Haynes ran down the list of his physical injuries: A large cut on his ankle, a bruised sternum, a bruised rib, a concussion, lacerations to both ears that took dozens of stitches to repair.

He confesses embarrassment that he never felt an ache. Nothing ever hurt. He didn't feel injured and, if not for the doctors' obvious concern about his concussion, felt mentally prepared to return to work almost immediately upon his release from the hospital. But even more than his lack of serious physical injury, his rare ability to emotionally move past the event seemed incredible to me. Certainly his initial instinct at the scene, that he'd been responsible for massive death, must have been a strong one. So I wondered aloud how he negotiated that transition from guilt to acceptance. And he repeated the theme continually woven through our conversation: Talk.

"I woke up and the hospital psychologist, Dr. Panisi, was holding my hand and started talking about the crash," he recounted. "I felt like I'd just killed 112 people and I didn't want to talk about it. That's the way I thought. I went down to see the crew the next day and the first thing I said was we won't talk about the crash, because I wanted us to give the NTSB each individual version of what happened, not our combined version. I wouldn't talk to anybody about the crash. I didn't look at the news, read the newspapers or do anything else. But eventually the psychiatrist got me talking about it. So there was that and all the other therapy I got, plus all the people who came to my room. I think everybody in Sioux City came to my room while I was in the hospital. I might as well have had a revolving door. They all came in and helped me talk about the crash. I'm almost embarrassed to say I don't really feel like I dealt with most anything, because I had so much support. They all convinced me we did everything we could in the airplane.

"About the third day as I remember, my wife, Darlene, is standing beside the bed and they're showing the news and they show the crash, and I ask her what crash that was. It's the first time I'd seen the crash, and I was convinced that there was absolutely no way anybody got out of that, and I knew at the time 185 had survived."

I told Haynes that I'd seen the videotape an hour and a half after the crash. I'd taken an ambulance from the runway to a holding area where other passengers who hadn't been badly injured were congregated. There was a television set there, broadcasting the news, and it showed this incredible airplane crash and I started wracking my brain trying to remember what famous aviation disaster they were showing, because it just wasn't familiar. Then someone told me it was us.

"Of course," Haynes said, "you've seen it a zillion times since. I was told by ABC that's the most viewed piece of news film ever, followed by the Challenger disaster. Oprah just showed it again about two months ago."

Haynes found himself portrayed in a dramatic version of United 232, a made-for-television docudrama that took very few liberties with the actual events — partly because much of the inflight dialogue was lifted directly from the cockpit tapes. It was called "A Thousand Heroes" and focused on the Sioux City rescue efforts. He had no quarrel with the casting. Charlton Heston played Al Haynes, defining his character with the powerful charisma that the actor has always brought to his roles. Some time after the movie had aired, a little girl who'd watched it was introduced to the real Al Haynes. "That's not him," she insisted.

"Heston's character is whatever he wants it to be, because he's never played anybody who hasn't been dead at least 100 years," Haynes said, laughing. "He wrote me a letter and said that. So he can do anything he wants. He can be Moses any way he wants to be Moses."

For me, the real Al Haynes was no disappointment, even if he came up a little short of Heston's Biblical proportions. The first time I met him in person was a few months after the crash at a support group meeting in Denver, a gathering in the clubhouse of an apartment complex where another survivor lived. Already, the captain had risen to heroic status in my eyes and the opportunity to shake his hand seemed something to savor.

I was standing in the back of the room when I saw him arrive. It must have been 40 minutes or so before I worked my way next to him and introduced myself, mumbling something about what a pleasure it was to finally meet him. I'll never forget the first thing he said to me: "How'd you ever go back into that plane?"

I can't recall my response. But I realized how deeply he cared about the people in that room, how familiar he'd become with our individual stories just as we'd grown to know him through so many media accounts of the crash. Going into the meeting, I'd felt a slight discomfort rooted in the fact that relatives of some victims would also be there, and the thought crossed my mind that the potential existed for things to turn ugly if some sought to tag Al Haynes as the scapegoat for the loss of a loved one. But the reality became just the opposite once he spoke, once they saw his personality and realized that he truly had done everything in his power to keep a doomed plane from charting a course toward even greater tragedy.

At the start of the meeting, a widow of one of the victims had told me about her unresolved anger toward Haynes. Afterward, I watched her hug him for what seemed an eternity. Our pilot was certainly heroic, but to me his most remarkable trait surfaced after the crash, when we witnessed his humanity.

"I don't like the word hero," Haynes said. "My definition of hero, and here's where it fits you and doesn't fit me, is someone who voluntarily puts himself in danger to help somebody else. You can bet your life we didn't voluntarily put ourselves in that airplane in that condition. I think the word is very overused. ABC-TV called me to do an interview on how you handle the publicity, because Scott O'Grady, that pilot shot down over Bosnia and then rescued, was getting all that publicity about being a hero. My answer to that is just don't believe it. As long as you don't believe it yourself, you're OK. And I've got all kinds of things to keep me from believing it, like when I go out to umpire a Little League game. I get brought back to earth right away."

Haynes became close to many of the survivors. He took more than a casual interest in the way our lives played out afterward. I felt honored when he invited me and my wife to accompany him on his last flight before his mandatory retirement at age 62.

It was a flight from Denver to Seattle, and much of the crew was the same as it had been on United 232. Records and Dvorak had moved on to different assignments with the airline and no longer were qualified to fly the DC-10, but they sat in jump seats. All the surviving flight attendants were on board, at the same stations they'd occupied on 232. Even three members of the rescue team from Sioux City were there.

I sat in the same seat, 23G. But this time, Diane was sitting next to me. The entire celebration became something of a media event, with press conferences and coverage on both ends of the flight. In Seattle, a ceremonial taxi beneath arching water sprays from fire department hoses had been arranged. The flight into Sea-Tac Airport was blessedly uneventful, but the arrival proved memorable.

"We're on our way down and we land. We taxi off the runway and there's three rings on the gong in the cockpit, which means there's a problem in the back end," Haynes recounted. "There's a guy in the back suffering diabetic shock. He can't breathe. The crew from Sioux City is working on him, and they tell me we've got to get an ambulance to the gate and get there right now. So we shot past those fire trucks like they weren't even there and taxi up to the gate. The ambulance is there, the police are there, the press. And they were carrying this poor guy down the stairs. Fortunately, it turned out he was fine. I might be a little blasphemous here, Jerry, but I believe the comment you made about me was something like: 'Gee, can't he land without an ambulance waiting for him?'"

He was right. That's exactly what I told the media, tongue in cheek, when we walked into the airport terminal. Again, we laughed at the way humor sometimes pops up when you least expect it.

My life had gone through emotional pitches and rolls, like our DC-10 that seemed to have a mind of its own and a destination wholly beyond our control. Haynes' life, while seemingly untouched by the emotions that haunted some other survivors, had assumed an unexpected trajectory that now took him all over the world to speak on the lessons of United 232 — a slice of aviation history that, when you boiled it down to basics, none of us completely understood. The important thing, it seemed, was first to acknowledge that lack of understanding.

"The only way to really explain it is what we did just happened to be the right thing at the right time," Haynes said. "The guys who have tried it in the flight simulator since then, they know what we did and they tried it. It didn't work. Maybe they waited a second too long, maybe they went two seconds too soon. Whatever we happened to try, happened to be exactly at the right time. There's no explaining why it worked. It didn't add up. We never should've gotten that far. As soon as that engine blew, and that airplane started to turn over, it should've gone upside down. We should've gone down like that" — and here, he stabbed the back of his fork sharply toward what remained of his pancakes — "and that should've been the end of it right there. How the airplane kept flying for 45 minutes, to this day, I can't answer."

No one could. Haynes said the NTSB wanted him and his crew to recreate the United 232 scenario on a flight simulator after the fundamental design defect had been corrected by the installation of a hydraulic fuse. He had two more DC-10 proficiency checks coming up in Denver, but the first time when he was asked to pilot the plane's modified version through the scenario he simply declined. During his last proficiency check he softened his stand somewhat and decided that maybe he'd try it. He had all but decided to give it a go. But first, he needed to finish the standard phase of the proficiency check.

"So we're doing this approach," he recalled, "and we come to the outer marker. If anything goes wrong from the outer marker in, you go around for another landing. For some reason, we don't know why, this ground proximity warning went off inside the outer marker. So there's one of five things you're doing wrong that could be dangerous. You're supposed to immediately go around. So we went around, came back in and landed. As we're walking in to have coffee, the instructor said, 'I was on radio. Do you know what you said when you called me and told me you were going around?' I said no. He said, 'You said, "*United 232* going around." I said I did not. He said yes you did, and he played the tape back and I sure as hell did. So I thought maybe I better not try to recreate the Flight 232 scenario."

When it comes to beating the odds, sometimes once is enough.

Chapter
10

BIRTH AND
REBIRTH

I suspect that all of us who survived the crash of United 232 found fragments of the wreckage turning up in our lives at unexpected times, just as Al Haynes learned in the flight simulator. Part of learning to deal with the effects of the crash involved coming to grips with the idea that this was not a memory that would fade away. The key, it seemed, was finding an anchor secure enough to keep us from drifting into dangerous waters.

For some that anchor might have been a spouse, or a job, or even an avocation like Haynes' public speaking. For others, like myself, it was a spiritual discovery that did not come quickly or easily. Diane's simple challenge had taken ten months to materialize — almost a year of denial and frustration. It was as if the recipe for resolving my survival had required that many specific ingredients be added slowly to the pot and left to simmer and stew. There was no microwaveable solution.

But once I felt the barriers come down, life clearly moved in a positive direction. Where once there had been the constant sensation of spiraling downward, there now was a solid sense of forward movement. Still, I scheduled another appointment with the trauma counselor, who had suggested that we follow up on our first meeting, when she diagnosed my depression and offered the Prozac alternative.

As I drove to the second appointment, I wondered how my new-found feelings of strength and well-being would be received in a clinical setting, and whether they would be dismissed by a mental health professional as smoke and mirrors, some kind of hocus-pocus of self-deception.

As we sat in her office, I explained what had happened, detailing that defining moment when Diane had said, "I get my strength from God," and the emotions that eventually sorted themselves out and left me feeling re-energized and completely changed.

It did not sound very scientific in the retelling. In fact, it sounded almost hokey, especially when I talked about the amazing physical strength that came over me as I sat in the bedroom chair. Yet when I finished my story I saw that the counselor's eyes had watered, as if what I'd said had struck some kind of personal chord and she was holding back tears. I waited for her to say something.

"No one," she finally said, "who goes through something like you did can ever reach the point where it's not there anymore. But in your case, you'd never be as healthy as you can be until you put God in your life. I can't tell *every* patient that, but I know it's true for you."

I don't know that I needed any clinical stamp of approval, but it was incredibly encouraging to hear someone trained in the science of the human mind acknowledge the power of what had happened to me. But I also knew that no matter how she reacted to my finding the Lord, I was not going to be changed. I was on the right path and I knew it. I was never going back to a life without God.

My visit had been scheduled for an hour, but after about 20 minutes I was saying good-bye and thank you to the counselor. She told me if I felt that I needed to come back to simply call, but we both knew that my worst days were behind me.

Still, that didn't mean I knew exactly where I was headed. It had been Diane's words that had started me in this direction, so naturally I sought her advice about what came next. She didn't want to disturb this sudden spiritual momentum, but she also knew that I would basically have to find my own way. And besides, she had heard me say many times that I had things under control. I could hardly blame her if she had some doubts about the authenticity of this drastic change.

But the compulsive organizer in me, the former quarterback, needed a game-plan to proceed. So I asked Diane what she thought my next step should be. Read the Bible? Talk to a priest? But she didn't want to push things along too fast.

Eventually, Diane gave me a copy of a book called The Hiding Place by Corrie ten Boom. It tells a compelling story of concentration camp survival and unchanging spiritual strength. Strangely enough, it was while reading this book that I was struck by a quotation from the Bible that ten Boom referred to many times, a passage from the book of Matthew. I'd surely heard the verse before, though it had never come home to roost quite like it did under these circumstances. "Come to me, all who are burdened and heavy laden, and I will give you rest."

The passage was, almost literally, the answer to my prayers. It occurred to me that when I prayed in the midst of my depression it was not for a job, a career, or that my marriage be salvaged. It was for relief, pure and simple. It was for rest.

There were, of course, practical as well as spiritual matters to consider at this time. Namely, I needed a job. A few interesting and flattering possibilities trickled in. I interviewed with the NBA's Portland Trailblazers for a marketing position, but afterward felt that the job wouldn't be right for me and took myself out of the running. A couple of agents who represented players I'd dealt with in the CBA called to see if I might be interested in joining them, but the player-agent business is an often unscrupulous world that seemed even less right for me. Another call came in from the Arena Football League inquiring if I might be interested in becoming commissioner, but that job, which seemed similar to the one I'd just quit, held no big attraction. But sportscasting still did, and I decided to focus my efforts in that area.

I wrote to a New York agency, Athletes and Artists, to see if they could help me find a broadcasting position. After I sent them some tapes of my work, they took me on as a client. In the meantime, Denver's radio sports talk was undergoing a lot of changes, sort of a domino effect of job openings that began when former football star and longtime local sports hero Dave Logan jumped AM stations, from KYBG to KOA, where he would have a role in the Denver Broncos broadcasts. I applied for the vacancy at KYBG that would involve delivering morning sports reports and co-hosting a mid-day call-in show. Although it was not play by play, it was radio sports and it was in a major market.

Meetings with the station's general manager, Ron Jamison, went well and by the middle of July we appeared to be on the verge of striking a deal as Diane and I boarded an airplane. It was July 18, 1990, and we were on our way to Sioux City for a memorial of the crash of United 232.

I was supposed to call Jamison to see if we could seal the deal, and when we landed in Lincoln, Nebraska, for a brief stopover I found a pay phone and made the connection. My duties at the station had not been fully outlined and neither had my salary. Diane and I had talked about this opportunity and come to two conclusions. One was that I would be flexible on the duties. And the other was that I would be flexible on the salary. The final negotiations, over the phone at the airport in Lincoln, were pretty straightforward. Jamison offered me specific duties and a specific salary, and I said yes.

It felt fantastic to be back among the employed, particularly as such good news came on the eve of the one-year anniversary of the crash.

As I hung up the phone and turned to start toward the gate, I ran straight into Al Haynes and two of the flight attendants who'd been aboard United 232 They, too, had a stopover in Lincoln before flying into Sioux City on the same flight we'd booked. It's always good to see people like Haynes and the crew that worked so diligently under such difficult conditions, but seeing them as I hung up the phone from accepting a new job seemed to bring things full circle in a positive sense.

As we all got on the plane for the final leg of the journey back to Sioux City, I felt remarkably good. One year after the crash I was doing all right, in spite of the troubles that had dogged me for most of the preceding months. I had come to grips with my depression. I'd found a spiritual direction that, though still barely defined, already had changed my life. I'd found a job. And as I felt the warm weight of Diane's head leaning against my shoulder while she dozed on the final leg of our journey, I also realized that I'd rediscovered the most important person in my life.

A feeling that bordered on euphoria settled over me as the plane landed smoothly on the runway at Sioux Gateway Airport, in stark contrast to the way I had arrived almost a year earlier. This strange emotional high didn't quite seem right, and it wasn't. After we'd landed safely, the euphoria evaporated and more familiar and difficult emotions returned. There I was, thinking that the incident was totally behind me, and the memorial hit me square in the face with the fact that United 232 will never be completely over and done.

Officials shut down the airport for a half-day on the morning of the memorial so survivors and families of the dead could roam the grounds, regain their bearings and explain to loved ones what had happened.

A minibus took a group of us out to the runway under dreary skies and let us out near the spot where our DC-10 had first touched down. The huge gouge in the concrete had been filled in and someone had placed a bouquet of flowers close by. Diane and I started there and walked slowly down the runway while I tried to explain the sequence of events, hoping that by bringing her to this spot where I could actually show and tell my story she would perhaps come to understand it more fully. I wanted to spill everything to her, yet I didn't want to upset her. She insisted on knowing the facts, on hearing my description while she stood on the very spot were my life had begun a long skid that had taken us to such depths in the past year.

For some reason, I did not get terribly emotional as I recounted the crash. It seemed almost as if I were telling someone else's story. We held hands the entire time as we retraced the plane's path down the runway, and I showed her where it veered into the cornfield and where I came out. I saw tears on Diane's face that slowly blended with the beginnings of a steady drizzle. We headed back to the bus and climbed aboard, still clutching each other's hands.

Later that morning, Diane and I headed over to Briar Cliff College, where I'd been asked to appear at a press conference. Mark and Lori Michaelson were there and so was Al Haynes and his wonderful wife Darlene. And so was Spencer Bailey, who was 4 years old at the time of the crash, which killed his mother. His father had brought him back to the memorial as a means of healing, of showing his son that Sioux City could be, in his words, "a place of mending as well as catastrophe." That hope was echoed by us all. Spencer had become known throughout the nation when his picture appeared in dozens, maybe hundreds, of newspapers and magazines. The photo showed him being carried from the scene of the crash by Col. Dennis Nielsen of the Iowa Air National Guard. It was a stirring sight, and it became the inspiration for a slate carving eventually erected in Sioux City to honor the rescue effort. Almost as stirring were the words Nielsen offered at that time when he was asked how he'd saved the little boy: "God saved the child, I just carried him out." That had more than a little meaning for me. It was exactly the way I felt about Sabrina Michaelson.

At the press conference, I sat next to Spencer and gazed at the burn marks still visible on his arm and neck, hoping that the scars ran no deeper for him. Looking at Spencer, I didn't even realize that tears had started to run down my face.

In the memorial service late that afternoon, I sat next to a woman who had survived the crash with her son. If I had already started to come down from the high that had seized me on the flight into Sioux City, then my conversation with this woman — or more specifically her words to me — brought me immediately back to earth. "I know I'll never again lead a normal life," she said matter-of-factly. "My marriage, my sex life, my relationship with my son, none of it is the same. It never will be. We can never go back to the innocence we had before 232."

Although I was somewhat shocked by what she said, I also knew that in many ways she was right. I had gotten carried away by my own sudden turn of good fortune. How many people get spiritual renewal and a new job within a couple months? It was true that I had made major strides forward emotionally, and the one-year memorial put a measure of closure on the memory of the crash itself. Still, it was naive to think that I was home free, just as it was foolish to imagine that an anniversary get-together could perform the kind of magic many of us probably imagined it would. The real test, I realized then, would not be how we made it through July 19 every year. The real test would be how we made it through the other 364 days.

The crash had revealed itself as an unshakable constant in my life, and I needed other constants to counterbalance it. Some of them I knew. Some had yet to arrive. And one showed up on the front page of the <u>Des Moines Register</u> the day after the memorial.

A photographer at the press conference had caught me in the middle of thinking about Spencer Bailey, when the tears had started to fall. There was nothing special about that. You could have closed your eyes and pointed a camera in any direction that day and caught someone shedding a tear. But what struck me about the photograph was something I hadn't remembered about that moment, something I had come to take for granted.

Diane had been seated next to me, and had raised her right hand to my cheek to wipe away those tears. She was smiling slightly, all comfort and understanding. For some reason I had no vivid recollection of that instant until I saw the newspaper.

I don't think I have ever seen Diane look more beautiful, in all the ways that really matter, than she does in that photograph. If I had felt a sense of well-being flying in to Sioux City, when she'd rested her head against my shoulder, then I felt something more solid when we flew back after the memorial. No matter where the effects of the crash took me, toward spiritual light or the darkest nightmares, Diane would be there — as a wife, as a friend, as a constant. One day, I hoped, she would also be there as a mother.

We had talked about having children just prior to the crash, but the subject got put on hold when the aftershocks started to drive a wedge between us. But not long after the one-year memorial, we started talking about it again. So much seemed to be happening in our lives, so quickly, that it was only a matter of time before the issue of family came up.

Only two months after I started work at KYBG, I'd gotten a call from Athletes and Artists saying that the Minnesota Timberwolves, second year members of the expanding NBA, were looking for a play-by-play announcer. In early October, I sent them a tape. A few days later, they flew me in to Minneapolis for a round of interviews with, among other people, a rising young sports executive named Tim Leiweke. In short order, I had a job doing play-by-play for 34 televised games and backing up their regular radio guy for another 26 games. It had finally happened — I was going to live my nearly lifelong dream of being an NBA announcer. The many years of sacrifice and frustration finally paid off.

The first NBA broadcast I did was on the radio, a Timberwolves exhibition game in Charlotte against the Hornets on October 22, 1990. I was a bit nervous, but I was also ready. I thought the broadcast went well and the production folks back in Minneapolis told me they thought it was great. After returning to my hotel room, I called Diane. She cried as I described the broadcast and the feelings I'd had before, during and after the game. When we hung up, I went to the hotel bar and ordered two beers — one for me and the other for Diane. Even though she wasn't there, I clinked the glasses in a toast. It was only right to share my triumph with the person most responsible for it.

We packed up and moved to Minnesota in time for the start of the regular season. By Christmas, we were making the drive to Topeka to spend the holidays with Diane's relatives and, as the interstate rolled past, talking about a baby. We felt the repercussions of the crash were no longer an issue, at least not in terms of our physical and emotional ability to raise a child. The only thing that gave us pause was the uncertainty of my job. I'd signed a one-year deal in Minnesota, and depending on how the chips fell after the season, there was no telling where we might end up. We resolved to let things be and see what happened after my first year calling the Timberwolves' games.

Professionally, the season went fine. Although the team suffered through the same pathetic performances any new team endures, it was a thrill to have finally reached the NBA level. But soon, personal tragedy struck again.

169

Toward the end of the season, my oldest sister Heidi's husband, Beau Bench, developed blood clots in his lungs. His condition became so dire that he checked into the renowned Mayo Clinic in Rochester, just an hour and a half south of Minneapolis. I made the drive there the morning he checked in and stayed with my sister for two days. After it appeared that Beau had stabilized, I returned to Minneapolis, but almost immediately my sister phoned and asked me to return. Heidi was trained as a nurse and she knew only too well what was happening to her husband and how serious his condition had become. The afternoon I arrived back in Rochester, I was met again by my sister as well as Beau's sister, Georgia, who had flown in from Alabama.

Beau slid downhill rapidly that same afternoon. My sister, sensing that the end might be near, called some friends in Sioux Falls, South Dakota, where she and Beau lived, and asked them to drive their two children, Eric and Allison, to Rochester, about a three hour drive. They didn't make it in time. Beau Bench was only 40 when he died.

My association with the Timberwolves continued for another year, but the new deal involved only television games, as internal politics left me the odd man out on the radio broadcasts. That was a bitter pill to swallow, but that's how the broadcast business works. It's not always what you know, but who you know. Tim Leiweke, who'd been one of my biggest backers in getting the Minnesota job in the first place, didn't have quite enough sway to keep me on the radio broadcasts. Eventually, he left the Timberwolves himself not long afterward to take a job in the front office of the Denver Nuggets. Since I would be doing only about 35 games for the T-wolves, Diane and I decided it would make sense for us to move back to Denver. I could commute easily for the broadcasts. Besides, we missed the city and the circle of friends that we'd developed over our years there and I figured I could find a part-time sportscasting job there. So in the summer of 1991 we headed back to the Rocky Mountains and I eventually got some part-time work with KOA radio to augment our income.

It was during my second year doing the Timberwolves that more pain came into our lives. About half way through the season, I returned home from a trip to the Twin Cities and Diane, as she often did, picked me up the airport. When we got to the car, she said she had a "special treat" for me and handed me a bag of Pepperidge Farm cookies. I thought it was a nice gesture on my wife's part, though a bit odd because I don't eat too many sweets. What I didn't notice was that these particular cookies were labeled "Dakotas." In our discussions about having children, we had both decided we liked the name Dakota for a boy. Diane was trying to tell me she was pregnant, but I completely missed the message. She finally had to come right out and say it. But the incredible joy, excitement and anticipation of becoming parents soon came to an abrupt halt. A couple weeks later, Diane suffered a miscarriage.

Although we never heard a heartbeat or even saw a glimpse of this tiny human being on an ultrasound picture, we mourned its passing. And we tried so hard to figure it out. How could God keep doing this to us? First a plane crash, then Beau's death and now a miscarriage.

But as difficult as that period was, six months later we once again found ourselves thinking about a child. Diane's physical signals pointed toward pregnancy, but we didn't dare get our hopes up. The emotional crash had been hard to overcome. So we waited a few weeks, thinking maybe her body had sounded a false alarm, and tried to keep our lives on an even keel. But finally, we had to know. Diane bought a home pregnancy test one day and disappeared into the bathroom. A short while later she emerged holding the piece of cardboard that changes color to indicate whether it's time to repaper a bedroom or go back to the drawing board. I'm sure I looked at it, but I can't for the life of me remember what color it was. I must have been blinded by the light from Diane's face, which was practically beaming through tears of relief and happiness.

A trip to the doctor confirmed what the home test had already told us. We were expecting. Where the cycle of life and death was concerned, it seemed we'd been hit pretty hard with death over the previous two years — Jay Ramsdell and 111 others on flight 232, my brother-in-law and then Diane's miscarriage. It was refreshing and renewing to be only months away from welcoming a baby into our lives.

This time Diane's pregnancy went according to plan, although her morning sickness should have been renamed 'morning, noon and night' sickness. And while we prepared for that wonderful upheaval on the home front I experienced another upheaval on the job. This time, for the better.

Once again, one move in the Denver radio market triggered a domino effect. The city had just been awarded a major league baseball expansion franchise, the National League's Colorado Rockies. KOA radio, my Denver employer, secured the team's broadcast rights and immediately went searching for a couple of play-by-play announcers. One of them was right under the station's nose. Jeff Kingery was a veteran of the Denver radio market who had always dreamed of doing major league baseball. While waiting years for the right opportunity, he had covered the NBA as the voice of the Denver Nuggets. Naturally, when KOA and the Rockies snapped him up, that left an opening for someone to step in and call the Nuggets games.

Technically, the new broadcaster would be hired by KOA, but with the team's approval. Since I was working part-time at the station already, I got wind of the changes early and wasted no time throwing my name into the hat. KOA already had more than a passing familiarity with what I could do behind the microphone, which surely worked in my favor. And it didn't hurt that Tim Leiweke, my Minnesota connection, now worked in the Nuggets' front office. I got the job.

By the start of the 1992-93 NBA season, it looked like things couldn't get much better for me. I had landed another pro basketball broadcasting gig — and the relative security of a three-year deal, no less — in the city where Diane and I both loved to live. And, most important, I was about to become a father.

We didn't want to know the baby's gender ahead of time, thinking it would be better to be surprised, and so we played the usual guessing game. Diane felt certain it was a boy, and the expectant mother's intuition usually holds true, from what I gathered talking to other parents. Yet for some reason, I thought she'd have a girl. Everyone says it doesn't matter, as long as the baby's healthy. That wasn't quite the way we felt. We felt that it didn't matter, period. If the baby was not healthy, we were still going to love the child with all we had. Boy or girl, healthy or unhealthy, it would be our child and we would try to be the best parents we could be.

When Diane finally showed the first signs of labor, we did what any reasonable couple expecting their first child would do. We went to a grocery store.

Actually, the reason for the trip was to register to vote in our county and that particular day happened to be the last day we could do so. Of course, we kept track of the contractions and did all the appropriate math. We knew we were a long way from delivery. And other shoppers, when their carts rolled past ours, frequently felt compelled to remark about Diane's condition. As we stood waiting in the check-out line, a checker at an idle register called a familiar question.

"When are you due?" she asked.

"In a few hours," Diane said calmly. "I'm in labor."

The checker's jaw dropped and her eyes widened, as if she feared my wife might give birth on the spot. What could she say then — "Paper or plastic?" But Diane explained that she was at least several hours away from motherhood. We got to the hospital in plenty of time for the delivery, which went smoothly. Easy

173

for me to say. I was just standing there, watching in wonderment and barking the occasional breathing directions we'd learned in our birthing class. Diane was doing all the work.

She did a terrific job. When Margaret Rae Schemmel came into the world it was as if every other concern that had burdened me over the last three years suddenly dissolved into irrelevance.

I caught my breath long enough to take the surgical scissors from the doctor and perform the ceremonial cutting of the umbilical cord.

At several points immediately after Maggie was born, Diane and I thought about all the different things our new daughter meant to us. Naturally, she meant the start of a real family, another generation, with all the attendant worries and hopes and dreams that go along with it. But she seemed so much more to us in the context of the previous three years. Diane talked, in the days and weeks after the birth, about the way God had worked. One child had been taken from us, for reasons we could never hope to fathom. And now another had been given to us. Diane often referred to them as "our babies," even though we never knew enough about the first to give it a name.

She also observed a certain balancing of the spiritual scales in the fact that while we had lost one child, God had spared another — Sabrina Michaelson — in the plane crash. That thought was comforting to me.

I found myself thinking about Beau Bench being taken from us, and imagined that Maggie somehow represented the next stage in the cycle of life and death and then life again. But I also thought about Evan Tsao, Sylvia's little boy who perished in the crash, and realized that balancing Maggie's birth against the tragedy visited upon others was a tricky proposition. Certain things about birth and death and the way they bump into our lives remain imponderable, and it isn't necessarily our place to figure them all out.

Back in Diane's hospital room, after Maggie had been examined thoroughly and cleaned up, a nurse brought our baby to be fed. Gradually our daughter fell asleep in her mother's arms. And then Diane drifted off as well.

In the hospital room, in an atmosphere of overwhelming peace, my thoughts drifted back to July 19, 1989.

I thought about the incredible sadness I had experienced onboard flight 232 with my belief that I would not live through the crash landing and thus would never become a father. The things I thought I would never see or do, Diane giving birth, my holding our own flesh and blood, I had just seen and done. Something I was convinced would never happen had just happened. I believed at that point there was no other person on earth more content or happier than I was.

Then something else came to mind. It was the Bible passage I had read so many times in the previous two years: "Come to me, all who are burdened and heavy laden, and I will give you rest."

After all I'd been through as a result of the crash of United 232, this time alone with Diane and our tiny little girl seemed like the ultimate spiritual oasis.

For a moment, it was as if the crash had never happened. In some way, however small, looking down upon Maggie's innocence let me reclaim a sliver of my own.

"This is the rest Jesus is talking about in that verse," I thought to myself. "This is the rest."

The promise had been kept.

A CORNFIELD
REVISITED

If there was a missing piece of the puzzle that had been my life since July 19, 1989, it seemed to be Sabrina Michaelson. I had been linked to the little girl in so many stories, so many news accounts that cast me as her life-saver, that I had come to believe that there should be some invisible bond between us, even though she'd been too young to have any lasting memory of me at the time of the crash.

When Mark Michaelson and I had our first awkward meeting at the Sioux City television station, he promised the family would stay in touch. And they did keep in contact. A couple months after the crash I got a call from Mark, asking Diane and me if we would join him and Lori for dinner at a restaurant in

Denver's Hyatt Regency Hotel. We were pleased to receive the invitation, but it seemed like we all felt a little self-conscious for the first ten or 15 minutes after we met at the hotel. Slowly, however, the dinner evolved into a pleasant get-together of four friends who found a lot to talk about beyond the obvious crash connection. But still, there seemed a lingering undercurrent — a self-consciousness on all sides that wouldn't quite go away. Walking to our cars afterward, I felt like I needed to say something to the Michaelsons. I didn't want it to sound presumptuous or falsely modest, but there seemed no way to communicate the message with any kind of finesse. So I just said it.

I said I didn't want them to feel like they owed me for what happened after the crash. I told them that I acted purely on instinct and that the only way to explain what happened was that it was God's work, and that if Sabrina had only a scratch on her face after surviving that ordeal, then she simply must have been destined to live. When I finished, Mark and I shook hands and he thanked me and both he and Lori seemed as relieved as I was to have confronted this awkward situation and lay it to rest.

I had no idea what, if any, sense of obligation the Michaelsons felt in the wake of all the media attention heaped upon me. All I knew for certain was that while I tried to cooperate with news outlets who contacted me, I never felt completely comfortable with the way the rescue story always seemed to come off, placing what I thought was disproportionate significance on my actions. It seemed quite possible to me that in some unintended way this burdened the Michaelsons, or at the very least put them in a difficult position where I was concerned. So in the parking lot, before we wished each other good-night, I tried to alleviate any awkwardness they might feel.

With that, my relationship with Sabrina Michaelson had been resolved — and then again, it hadn't. About a month later I received a note from Sabrina, who'd just turned one year old. "Thank you, Mr. Schemmel, for saving my life," one of her parents had written for her. "You're my knight in shining armor."

178

Then, before Christmas, we received a card from the Michaelsons with a picture of their little girl. On both of those occasions, I felt an emotional twinge as I opened the envelope and gazed at its contents, but the feeling was different from what I'd expected.

Intellectually, I reasoned that there would probably be some life-long bond between me and the baby I'd carried from the wreckage. But emotionally, that bond just didn't seem to be there. It wasn't that I didn't care about her or want to stay apprised of her development. It was more a case of unfulfilled expectations, an absence of something vivid and spectacular that tied us together. To be sure, the crash itself was still vivid and spectacular, at least in my mind, but I strained to feel more than I actually felt about my connection with this child — a connection that had been reinforced so strongly by the news media and by my willingness to tell and retell the tale. The story developed a life of its own, and I found myself watching and reading the accounts and, perhaps subconsciously, trying to make my true feelings somehow live up to the hype.

Part of the problem, and maybe the biggest part, was the "hero" label. It always felt artificial. It always felt somehow forced by circumstances so horrible that the media understandably seized whatever positive acts they could and portrayed them as almost larger than life. I happened to hear a baby cry, look for her and find her. It sometimes does occur to me how close I might have been to not hearing the cry, or not realizing in the confusion exactly what I had heard. The time for painstaking reflection had already come and gone during the 45 minutes between the engine's explosion and our touch-down in Sioux City, and all that remained after that was raw reaction. Once, when I tried to explain to a reporter that what I'd done to find Sabrina was just basic, unremarkable human instinct, and did not involve any particular deliberation, he replied: "Yeah, but you did it. I don't think I would have." The headline on an editorial in the Topeka Capital-Journal read: "Schemmel — Our Kind of Hero," and went on to say that I was a hero precisely because I didn't think I was

179

a hero. The more I denied the label, the more it seemed somebody tried to pin it on me.

As the effects of the crash settled over me in the weeks and months afterward, there were times when I truly wanted to feel like a hero, when it seemed like this one redeeming feature of an otherwise awful experience might ease the pain and the guilt. So I would replay it in my mind. But in the end, it always felt like something that just happened, as if I were simply the tool of some larger destiny.

That's not to say that whatever forces moved me to find Sabrina Michaelson did not eventually help in the healing process as I dealt with my personal trauma. But I came to regard the chain of events not as an act of bravery on my part, but as a genuine gift above and beyond my simple survival. I look back at all the people on that flight, so many of them killed or injured, and realize that I emerged with multiple blessings, not the least of these was the fact that I had been in the right place at the right time to carry a little girl to safety.

Perhaps one of the more positive things to come out of this so-called "hero story," or at least the way it was told on television and in newspapers and magazines, had almost nothing to do with me and little to do with the facts. I heard from many, many people that the accounts about me going back into the burning wreckage after Sabrina Michaelson had renewed their faith in the human spirit. Of course, this presupposed that my actions involved some split-second weighing of the risks, followed by a well-thought-out sprint back into the cabin.

If all that were true, then my own spiritual recovery probably would have progressed much faster. But it didn't seem to matter how often I explained that I'd done what I'd done without thinking. Somehow, I always wound up as the poster boy for the public's reinforced faith in humanity. This was not such a bad thing, I suppose, but I was constantly struck by the irony that the average newspaper reader might have felt a lot better about this story than I ever did.

Not long after the crash, an independent television production company arrived at my office in CBA headquarters to film an interview for a show called "Witness to Survival." It was a short-lived show about people who'd been in life-or-death situations. They decided to feature my experience with United 232 for their first show. The camera crew set up and I went about the business of describing what had happened, responding to questions along the way. We'd been taping for awhile when suddenly the photographer stepped away from his camera, his eyes red and wet. He said he had to stop. I felt bad that I'd upset him and interrupted the shooting, but he explained that "these are happy tears, because I have a new confidence in the human spirit."

At the lowest times of my life, when I couldn't pull myself above the depression brought on by the crash, how desperately I'd wished for some of that confidence in the human spirit. America seemed to be reveling in my so-called heroics while I slid farther and farther into an emotional funk. To me it was almost an accident that I went after Sabrina, utterly without premeditation. I heard a baby cry and the next thing I remember is I'm pulling away debris, digging toward the sound of her voice. I wasn't thinking about risking my life, I wasn't thinking about the fire. I wasn't thinking about the cabin exploding. In fact, it's as if the whole process involved no thought at all. As Captain Haynes said about the frenzied activity in the cockpit, we all just made it up as we went along.

I have thought about heroism a lot since then. Intrigued by the media's tendency to throw the word around so liberally, I attempted to reach some reasonable definition of my own. To me, the purest form of heroism does not involve a single act. It is not 10 or 20 seconds of instinctive reaction in the face of danger. It is instead an extended period of strength and integrity displayed in the face of adversity. Heroism, to me, is measured by how someone lives his life, by his everyday attitudes and actions, not by one particular action or event.

181

That definition came to me as I thought about the relatives of the people who died on United 232. They were the ones who had to find the strength to pick up the pieces of lives shattered by loss. They had to fill the emptiness left by a mother or father, a son or daughter, a husband or wife — any close relation who did not survive the crash. I lost a great friend and colleague, but my hurt heals in a way theirs probably never will. By simply moving forward with their lives, day by day by day, they set a standard for heroism that brief, random circumstance can never hope to duplicate. In my book, heroism is a process, not an act. The real heroes from flight 232 are the families of its victims.

As it turns out, this thread of so-called heroism I once assumed would bind me forever to Sabrina Michaelson simply did not exist. In my darkest hours following the crash, I tried to find comfort in the connection. But it wasn't there. Every Christmas, when the Michaelsons' card faithfully arrived in the mail, I would smile at the photograph of the toddler who gradually changed — already growing blonde and tall — and stick it on the refrigerator with a magnet until the next year's picture arrived. But the feeling I got when I looked at the child in the photo was never one of intense emotion, as if our souls had been linked by this single, monumental event in our lives. There was nothing so dramatic. It felt more like we were distant friends, growing more distant with every day that she grew toward maturity and I moved toward a fuller understanding of what had happened to me. She would probably never remember the crash and I would certainly never forget it. Our connection would probably be nothing more than a trail of newspaper clippings and the ritual Christmas card exchange.

For awhile this seemed a little bothersome. A part of me clung to the idea that there should be something more, even though I held the 11-month-old girl in my arms for probably less than five minutes. I hadn't seen her since that day and, as the years passed and the pictures on the refrigerator changed, I began to wonder whether it might be a good idea to see her in person. On the occasions I'd seen Mark and Lori, the kids had not come along, so it had been six years since I had actually been in her presence. I had no idea what to say to her or what to expect from Sabrina, at all of seven years old. But I suspected that for me, a reunion held the possibility of closure for another facet of the crash.

Sometimes, my recovery seemed like a constant progression of closure — addressing my physical condition, settling my legal claim, resolving guilt over Jay's death, ending my career with the CBA, picking Captain Haynes' brain about the goings-on in the cockpit. There was always something else to deal with, to put behind me. I thought perhaps Sabrina Michaelson might be next on the closure activity list.

On November 15, 1995, the Nuggets were scheduled to play a road game against the Phoenix Suns. I called Lori and Mark, who had relocated to the Phoenix area, a few weeks prior and asked them if they would like to attend. They said yes and I arranged to have two tickets waiting for them at America West Arena. They showed up soon after the doors opened and we were able to talk for 20 minutes or so before I began rehearsal for the television broadcast.

I remember sitting in the first row behind the scorer's table with Mark and Lori and thinking how ironic it was that we were doing so and nobody, outside of Nuggets media relations director Tommy Sheppard, who had helped me get their tickets, understood the significance of what was happening. For years, dozens of television producers as well as numerous newspaper and magazine writers had tried unsuccessfully to reunite me with the Michaelsons. The Michaelsons always said no, and for the same reason — privacy — that they preferred their family photos not appear in this book. And suddenly there we were together, with three local television stations doing live shots and dozens of other cameras roaming the arena because of a national network broadcast, and nobody recognized the reunion.

After the game, we chatted briefly again. Lori and Mark asked me when the Nuggets were playing in Phoenix again and mentioned that they'd like to have me over to the house for dinner and to see the kids. I told them our next game was December 29th, about a month and a half later, and we agreed that I would come to dinner at their house the night before the game.

As December 28 approached, I grew a little apprehensive about the dinner — and the reunion. There were two reasons for that.

One was my own state, my own sense of recovery from the crash. There was always the thought, more a fear actually, that something might leap into my life and suddenly disrupt that recovery. For a long time, I feared that the critical event would be a plane ride, that I might suddenly have a panic attack in the middle of heavy turbulence and never be able to fly again. But now the thought occurred that a reunion with Sabrina might be the event, that it might somehow throw a monkey wrench into my recovery. Even more important, I began to feel concern that a reunion might not be the best thing for Sabrina.

In Phoenix, on the morning before we were to meet for dinner, while out for one of my coveted distance runs, Lori Michaelson left a message on my hotel room's voice mail. She said she was sick with the flu and didn't feel up to going through with our dinner plans. As I listened to her message, I felt nothing but relief.

On my run, I'd thought deeply about how the night might go, and the question of whether it was the right thing for everyone concerned became a heavy one. But after hearing Lori's voice mail message, I hung up the phone with a strong, reassuring thought: I didn't *need* to see Sabrina Michaelson. I didn't *need* to have this reunion to end another chapter of recovery. I already had that means. I had Jesus Christ.

Through all the media coverage that dwelled on my rescue of Sabrina, I'd come to believe the relationship might contain some crucial element of my recovery, or at the very least that it remained an open door that needed closing. But what I came to realize was that most of the answers I'd sought after the crash could be discovered by looking inward, through an awakening of the spirit. The answers were not necessarily to be found in the people, places and things that orbited my life. The answers came through faith in God.

***

The Jay Ramsdell Memorial Game, a CBA exhibition to benefit a foundation that gives scholarships to high school kids from his home state of Maine, was scheduled for November 9, 1995 in Sioux City and I had agreed to say a few words before tip-off. I had no prepared speech to fill the few seconds I would have the microphone, just a few basic thoughts about what an honor it was to be there and how grateful I am to the entire city for its enduring friendship and, of course, its exemplary rescue effort.

My flight arrived late in the morning and I met Jay's dad at Briar Cliff College, where he sat in on my talk to the school's women's basketball team about surviving United 232 and its effects on my life. In the afternoon, I still had a few hours to kill before game time, so I drove to the flight 232 memorial sight that had been erected along the Missouri River in a park near downtown. I just sat there awhile, pondering all the same big questions, except this time with an underlying sense that some of them might already have been answered. Then, I drove to a grocery store, asked a bewildered clerk for a paper bag and, tossing it on the seat beside me in my rental car, headed out to the airport.

Maybe the airport was a sort of spiritual or emotional reference point, an arrow on the compass in my head or heart. For whatever reason, I went there and walked into the small terminal, headed for the restaurant, ordered a Diet Pepsi and found a seat where I could have a clear view of the runway.

So many things seemed so much clearer now than they had at any time in the previous six years. Looking out on the strip of concrete that appeared to have healed all its visible scars, I felt at peace.

The crash had pretty much carved out its place in my soul but at least I knew, through God's help, that it was there. I knew precisely where it was, knew its width and depth the way you come to know the deep pothole on the route home from work. And somehow, I had managed to fill the space around it with life. My own healing will probably never be complete, and there might never be that sense of total closure that so many of us survivors hoped for. But I had walked away with so much more than many of the others. I had my health, a loving wife and a beautiful young daughter. I had the career of my dreams, following an NBA team and calling its games on both radio and television. I lived in a city of exciting growth at the doorstep of vast natural beauty. And, most importantly, I had a spiritual awakening that was both humbling and strengthening.

After awhile, I got up from my seat and walked outside, along a chain-link fence, to the spot where the video camera had taped the crash sequence seen by millions of viewers on their television screens, and by many of us long afterward in our nightmares. The runway now looked almost serene in the late Iowa autumn. I headed to my rental car and drove down a road that runs alongside the runway toward a hangar where the tail section of our DC-10 had been stored for years, usually only half-covered by a tarp. While locations like the memorial and the airport jogged the memory and gave rise to meditation, this burned-out section of fuselage had always served as a grittier reminder of what happened here.

Gouged runways could be filled in, cornfields could be replanted and harvested in a never-ending cycle and tastefully conceived monuments could be unveiled, but the jagged frame of this piece of the airplane never failed to touch a nerve in me. It was tangible proof of the ordeal, an undeniable presence of past disaster. As time passed and the psychological fallout of the crash zoomed off on all sorts of wild tangents, that section of the plane brought the physical episode back with jarring clarity during the half dozen times I revisited Sioux City. It wasn't that I wanted to drive down to the hangar and have a peek. I needed to. And it was always there, a stark visual link to my past, its bones barely covered by the tarp. It was my skeleton in the closet.

Some part of me just assumed that it would be there forever, that after the irresistible force of our crash landing, it would become the immovable object — immovable, yet on some visits it would move me to prayer. But as I approached the hangar, that chunk of wreckage from the DC-10 was nowhere to be seen. My first sensation was slight alarm. This dark and accidental memorial had vanished, making the pilgrimage to the crash site an almost empty thing. I drove back to the terminal to ask what had happened to the last traces of United 232, and a maintenance worker told me it had been sold for scrap. It took awhile for that to sink in, but when it finally did, it felt right.

From the terminal I headed north on one of the gravel roads that runs alongside the airport, toward the cornfields. A high chain-link fence separated the road from the recently harvested stalks and I slowed the car in search of a patch of shoulder. When I found one, I pulled off and sat there, waiting for the sparse traffic to clear and clutching the paper bag I'd picked up at the grocery store. When no cars were visible in either direction, I got out and walked closer to the fence, wondering what would happen if anybody witnessed what I was about to do. Maybe I'd be arrested. Maybe I'd just be considered a confused visitor who was a few bricks shy of a load.

The idea had been gnawing at me for a long time. I'd always known that sooner or later I would return to the cornfield by myself — just walk out there amid the corn, or what was left of the stalks, to see how it felt. A few months earlier I'd even dreamed about wandering into the soft and familiar dirt and finding a piece of metal from the plane. And now here I stood, in the shirt and tie and dress slacks I would wear to the game that night, gathering the courage to scamper up the chain-link, negotiate the strands of barbed wire at the top and drop, dress shoes first, into the ditch that ran along the cornfield. It sounds now like some pointless prank, but in fact I felt very much like a man on a mission, prodded by the notion that this cornfield had taken a piece of me, and now I was going to claim a piece of it. That's why I took the paper bag along as I scaled the fence, miraculously managing not to shred my clothes on the barbed wire. The next thing I knew, my feet were planted in the cornfield. The eagle had landed.

I cast repeated glances toward the dirt road to reassure myself that no passing cars had seen my impromptu, and possibly illegal, crossing. Satisfied that no one had, I took several strides out into the remnants of that season's crop and just stood there, drinking it all in. I could tell by looking at the terminal in the distance that I was close to exactly the spot where my piece of the plane ended up — perhaps no more than 100 yards away.

Of course, it was different now. In mid-July, the corn had been tall, and those of us who survived the crash wandered through the rows as if lost in a maze and unable to get our bearings. In mid-November, with the harvest in, the visual barriers were eliminated and the field could be seen in its true context, creeping harmlessly to the edge of the airport property. It seemed less mysterious this way. Instead of the surreal and almost hypnotic pattern of tall, green rows that disoriented many of us after we scrambled from the DC-10's wreckage, there was now just a dull, vast blanket of brown and black.

In a way, my immediate feeling was similar to what I'd felt less than an hour earlier, when I'd looked for the piece of fuselage by the hangar and found nothing. It was an almost involuntary sense of alarm at the change, but that quickly passed and finally the cornfield looked and felt like nothing but a cornfield. The connection I'd expected to feel, like some invisible line through time and space binding me forever to this spot, simply wasn't there.

I kicked some dirt around and tried to remember what it had been like after the crash, but too much had changed. I don't know whether it was the difference in the way things looked on the outside or if it had more to do with changes that had taken place on the inside, within me, but I couldn't stir up the kind of emotion I thought I'd feel when I imagined scaling the fence and sneaking into the field.

But there I was, paper bag in hand, and there was no telling when I'd be back again, if ever. So I bent down and scooped some dirt into the bag. It had all seemed so serious in the planning, but now it felt kind of nutty. But at the same time, it felt good.

I could not have foreseen that, only a few weeks later, I would pick up a copy of a book called Rise and Walk, the story of pro football player Dennis Byrd's heroic battle to walk again after breaking his neck in a game. In the book he talks about growing up and playing football in small-town Oklahoma and, when he moved on to greater things and bigger stadiums, how he took a coffee can full of dirt gathered from outside the trailer house he grew up in and ceremonially sprinkled a handful on the field of each NFL stadium in which he played. So maybe my gesture wasn't so far off base after all.

When I finished scooping the dirt into my bag that was now about a quarter full, I looked up again to make sure that no one was watching before I headed back to the chain-link fence and repeated the awkward climb, hoping I would catch neither my pants nor the bag on the barbed wire. My mission accomplished, I returned to the rental car and placed the bag on the floor by the backseat. But for some reason, I wasn't ready to turn the key in the ignition and drive away. So I got out, walked around to the front of the car and sat on the hood. Feeling completely relaxed, I began assessing the ways my life had changed on this patch of ground and in the air above it.

My first thought was of the 112 who perished. I said a prayer for those who had come to rest in this place forever, and their families.

Eyes closed, I asked myself the same question I had asked hundreds of times over the previous six years: Why did I survive?

Even after all this time, the answers were not entirely clear, but a few things had become evident. Like Al Haynes, I felt compelled to share what had happened to me, to speak publicly about the crash and especially about the positive changes it had brought about in my life. But while the captain's talks stress human teamwork, mine stress a different teamwork. Mine are about a teamwork with God.

I knew that God tested me through this ordeal, and ultimately brought me to this point of peace and well-being, to serve as a living example — a living example that painful trials can bring about liberating personal change. I knew that I was chosen to live so that I may help bring others to Him.

Other random realizations found me beside the cornfield. Although I felt extremely fortunate to have reached my career goals, it seemed that my appreciation no longer centered on trivial things like money and notoriety so much as the simple satisfaction of doing a difficult job well. The basic value instilled by my parents, that people's true worth is defined by their character, had been doubly reinforced by my ordeal.

Others have asked, again and again, how the crash changed me. I think, in some ways, they were really asking a question about themselves, about the meaning of their own lives, and they looked to me as someone with a unique perspective, someone whose life was given back to him. And I realized I found it. Flight 232 allowed me to find life's real meaning, and it's really very simple. It's doing God's work. It's going in the direction God wants us to go, saying the things God wants us to say, doing the things God wants us to do. It's living the life God wants us to live.

And figuring out God's plan in our lives is also very easy. Just ask Him. He'll tell you.

In the final analysis, this pilgrimage to the corn was all about moving on from here. It was not about dirt, or reclaiming a piece of myself from the soil. The fact of the matter was the dirt held no particular meaning. Maybe some part of me wanted it to mean something, just the way I had wanted my tie to Sabrina Michaelson to feel like more than it was.

Still, I took the dirt home with me, thinking that perhaps I would carry this ritual one step further. I could mix the earth from the bag with the soil in the backyard where my family had sunk its figurative roots and then, on some fine day the following spring, take my daughter outside and plant flowers in the dirt that once nurtured the Iowa corn where her father had emerged into a life that would never be the same. But I left the brown bag on my work bench in the garage, which is a place where it can be easily overlooked, if never quite forgotten.

The legal actions, the media coverage, the guilt about Jay Ramsdell's death, the anger over the disquieting movie <u>Fearless</u>, the emotional numbness I later recognized as depression, the magnetic draw of the cornfield, the minutes-long relationship with Sabrina — all of these things were part of my search for resolution to the crash. Yet none really cut to the core.

The real reconciliation of the tragedy and the miracle that was United 232 happened for me exactly ten months after the crash, in the dim light of a bedroom as I sat slumped in a chair, at an emotional and spiritual low. It was when Diane spoke the words that were my turning point.

The real reconciliation of flight 232 was giving my life to God.

Flight 232 black box recording transcript:

3:23:31   Minneapolis
Radar Tower:

Sioux City, I have an
emergency for you. I have
a United aircraft coming
in . . . lost number two
engine . . . having a
hard time controlling
aircraft right now . . .
undecided Sioux City
right now.

Airport
Tower:

Radar contact

Aircraft:
(Captain)

You know we're having a
hard time. No
controllability, very little
elevator and almost no
control of aileron. I
don't think I can turn
right. I can only make left
turns.

Aircraft:
(First Officer)

You can't turn left.

Aircraft:
(Captain)

We can't turn left.

3:26:51	Airport Tower:	United 232; let me understand you sir. You can only make right turns.
3:26:57	Aircraft: (Captain)	Affirmative
3:27:13	Aircraft: (Captain)	OK, we're in a right turn now, it's about the only way we can go. We'll be able to make very slight turns on final but right now just we're gonna make right turns to whatever heading you want.
3:27:42	SAM:	United 232; this is SAM.
3:27:47	Aircraft: (Captain)	SAM, this is United 232. We blew number two engine and we've lost all hydraulics and we are only able to control, ah, level flight with the, ah, with the, ah, asymmetrical power settings. We have very little rudder or elevator.
3:28:03	Airport Tower:	United 232 heavy; fly heading two four zero and say your souls on board.
3:28:06	SAM:	Yeah, United, ah 232. Understand that you lost number two engine totally sir.

3:28:08	Airport Tower:	Souls on board United 232?
3:28:11	Aircraft: (Captain)	Getting that right now.
3:28:13	SAM:	Your, ah, system one and system three, are they operating normally?
3:28:16	Aircraft: (Captain)	Negative. All hydraulics are lost. All hydraulic systems are lost. Ah, the, ah, only, ah, thing we have is the air driven generator deplo . . . deployed . . . ah, we have normal . . . normal . . . engine power on one and three.
3:28:41	SAM:	OK . . . two . . . understand you have . . . normal power on one and three engines.
3:28:46	Aircraft: (First Officer)	Wonder about the . . . ah . . . outboard ailerons . . . if we put some flaps out you think that would give us outboard?
3:28:49	Aircraft: (Second Officer)	God I hate to do that.
3:28:50	Aircraft: (Captain)	Well, we're gonna have to do something.

3:28:52	SAM:	United 232; is all hydraulic quantity gone?
3:28:57	Aircraft: (Second Officer)	Ah . . . yes . . . all hydraulic quantity is gone.
3:28:59	Airport Tower:	United 232 heavy; say souls on board and fuel remaining.
3:29:14	SAM:	OK United, ah, 232 . . . what . . . what . . . what's . . . ah . . . where you gonna set down?
3:29:25	Aircraft: (Captain)	What's SAM doing?
3:29:27	SAM:	232.
3:29:29	Aircraft: (Second Officer)	Go ahead.
3:29:32	SAM:	United . . . ah . . . 232 . . . ah . . . where you gonna set it down?
3:29:37	Aircraft: (Second Officer)	We need some assistance right now. We can't . . . ah . . . we're having a hard time controlling it.
3:29:41	Aircraft: (Captain)	We don't have any controls.
3:29:43	SAM:	OK . . . United . . . ah . . . 232 . . . ah.

3:29:50	SAM:	I . . . I'll try to help ya . . . I'll pull out your flight manual.
3:29:54	Aircraft: (Second Officer)	I got the flight manual out. What do you want me to go to?
3:29:57	Aircraft: (Captain)	(to first officer) See what you can see back there will ya? Go back and look at the wing . . . and see what we got.
3:29:59	Aircraft: (First Officer)	OK.
3:30:00	SAM:	United 232; that's . . . ah . . . affirmative. We got to go to where we lose all hydraulic power.
3:30:04	Aircraft: (Second Officer)	Don't pull the throttles off.
3:30:06	Aircraft: (Captain)	Don't get too lost. It's all immaterial.
3:30:12	Aircraft: (Second Officer)	OK. The checklist . . . I could find on that . . . ah . . . there's the one and three or one and . . . ah . . . two and . . . I don't have anything for loss of all hydraulics.
3:30:44	Aircraft: (Captain)	You got hold of SAM?

3:30:46	Aircraft: (Second Officer)	Yeah, I've talked to em.
3:30:56	Aircraft: (Captain)	We're not gonna make the runway fellas. We're gonna have to ditch this son of a bitch and hope for the best.
3:31:15	Aircraft: (Second Officer)	OK. We're . . . ah . . . we don't know what we'll be able to do. We don't . . . ah . . . think we're even gonna be able to get on the runway right now. We have no control hardly at all. We need any help we can get from SAM as far as what to do with this. We don't have anything, we don't know what to do. We're having a hard time controlling it. We're descending. We're down to seventeen thousand feet. We have . . . ah . . . hardly any control whatsoever.
3:31:52	Aircraft: (Captain)	How are they doing on evacuation?
3:31:54	Aircraft: (Training Pilot)	They're putting things away, but they're not in any big hurry.

Appendix

3:31:57	Aircraft: (Second Officer)	Well, we can't make Chicago. We're gonna have to land somewhere out here, probably in a field.
3:32:03	SAM:	United 232; we have to land near the nearest airport. The nearest airport . . . ah . . . I'm trying to find out where you've lost all three hydraulic systems.
3:32:05	Aircraft: (Captain)	Well, they better hurry. We're gonna have to ditch I think. I don't think we're gonna make the airport.
3:32:14	Aircraft: (Training Pilot)	No. We got no hydraulics at all.
3:32:15	Aircraft:	(sound of warning horn)
3:32:18	Aircraft: (Training Pilot)	Get this thing down. We're in trouble.
3:32:20	Aircraft (Captain)	(to airport tower) Sir, we have no hydraulic fluid which means we have no elevator control, almost none, and very little aileron control. I have serious doubts about making the airport. Have you got someplace

near there that we might
be able to ditch? Unless
we get control of this
airplane, we're gonna put
it down wherever it
happens to be.

3:32:32   SAM:

United 232. Have you lost
all manual flight control
systems?

3:32:36   Aircraft:
           (Second Officer)

That's apparently true.

3:32:38   SAM:

United . . . ah . . . United
. . . ah . . . 232 . . . ah . . . in
the flight manual . . . in
the flight manual . . . one
sixty three, one sixty
three.

3:32:43   Aircraft:
           (Second Officer)

I'm on one sixty three.

3:33:06   Aircraft:
           (Captain)

This is Sioux City, Iowa.
That's where we're
headed.

3:33:09   Aircraft
           (First Officer)

Sioux City. There's no
DME. Nothing. I'm not
getting anything out of it.

3:33:14   Aircraft:
           (Training Pilot)

Got you on radar. You get
on number one and ask
them what that . . . where
the hell we are.

3:33:16	Aircraft: (Captain)	(to airport tower) Where's the airport now . . . ah . . . for 232 as we're turning around in circles?
3:33:21	Airport Tower:	United 232 heavy; ah, say again.
3:33:24	Aircraft: (Captain)	Where's the airport to us now as we come spinning down?
3:33:27	Airport Tower:	United 232; the airport's about twelve o'clock and three six miles.
3:33:32	Aircraft: (Captain)	We're trying to go straight. We're not having much luck.
3:33:40	Aircraft: (Captain)	Soon as the nose starts up we have to push forward on the yoke.
3:33:48	SAM:	United 232, I'm . . . I'm getting . . . ah . . . er . . . contact with flight ops right now. Standby please.
3:33:58	Aircraft: (Captain)	We kinda got level flight back.

3:34:09	Aircraft: (Captain)	(laughter) . . . we didn't do this on my last proficiency check.
3:34:12	Aircraft: (First Officer)	No.
3:34:16	Aircraft: (Captain)	Poured coffee all over.
3:34:18	Aircraft: (Training Pilot)	It's just coffee. We'll get this . . . this thing on the ground. Don't worry about it.
3:34:23	Aircraft: (First Officer)	It seems controllable, doesn't it Al?
3:34:26	Aircraft: (Training Pilot)	Yeah, the lower you get, the more dense that air is, the better your shots.
3:34:53	SAM:	United 232, this is SAM.
3:34:58	Aircraft: (Second Officer)	SAM, 232. We're going to try to put it in at . . . Sioux City.
3:35:05	Airport Tower:	232; understand you're going to try to make it to Sioux City.
3:35:15	Aircraft (Captain)	OK, we'll head for Sioux City. We got a little bit of control back now. How long's your runway?

3:35:19	Airport Tower:	The airport . . . ah . . . the runway is nine thousand feet long, a hundred fifty feet wide. And United 232 heavy, did you get the souls on board?
3:36:07	Aircraft: (Captain)	Tell you right now we don't even have time to let go to call the gal . . . ah . . . two ninety two.
3:36:27	Aircraft: (Training Pilot)	Nose is coming back.
3:36:33	Aircraft: (First Officer)	Yeah, we're going up.
3:36:40	Aircraft: (Training Pilot)	Power's coming back. Power's coming back.
3:36:52	Aircraft: (Captain)	We're just going to have to keep turning right. There's not much we can do about left. We'll try to come back around to the heading.
3:36:56	Aircraft: (First Officer)	Is this Sioux City, down to the right?
3:38:40	Aircraft: (Training Pilot)	I'll tell you what. We'll have a beer when this all done.
3:38:44	Aircraft: (Captain)	Well, I don't drink, but I'll sure as hell have one.

203

3:39:54	Airport Tower:	United 232, you think you'll be able to hold about a two forty heading?
3:39:57	Aircraft: (Captain)	We're trying to turn on it now.
3:39:59	SAM:	OK . . . ah . . . United 232 . . . I've got operational engineering on its way over and . . . ah . . . at the present time . . . ah . . . ah . . . at the present time . . . ah . . . ah . . . you . . . you're doing just about everything that . . . ah . . . you can possibly do.
3:40:04	Airport Tower:	When you get turned to that two forty heading, sir, the airport will be about, oh, twelve o'clock and thirty eight miles.
3:40:09	Aircraft: (First Officer)	OK. We're trying to control just by power alone now. We have no hydraulics at all so, ah, we're doing our best here.
3:40:15	Airport Tower:	Roger. We've notified the equipment out in that area too sir. The equipment here on the airport is standing by and they're sending some out to that area.

3:40:52	Aircraft: (Captain)	(to flight attendant) It's gonna be tough. Gonna be rough.
3:40:54:	Aircraft: (Flight attendant)	So we're gonna evacuate?
3:40:56	Aircraft: (Captain)	Well, we're gonna have the gear down.
3:40:58	Aircraft: (Flight Attendant)	Yeah.
3:40:59	Aircraft: (Captain)	And if we can keep the airplane on the ground and stop standing up, give us a second or two before you evacuate.
3:41:08	Aircraft: (Captain)	Brace. The brace will be the signal. It'll be over the PA system. Brace, brace, brace.
3:41:12	Aircraft: (Flight Attendant)	And that will be to evacuate?
3:41:14	Aircraft: (Captain)	No. That'll be to brace for landing. And then if we have to evacuate, you'll get the command signal to evacuate. But I think, really have doubts, you'll see us standing up, honey. Good luck sweetheart.

| 3:41:21 | Aircraft: (Flight attendant) | Thanks. You too. |

| 3:41:36 | Aircraft: (Training Pilot) | OK, I'm gonna try, I'm trying to hold you about two ten. I'll just see if makes a difference if I bump it, bump it up in the air. This may be the world's fastest tricycle. |

| 3:43:03 | Aircraft: (Captain) | (to airport tower) We're going to have to continue one more right turn. We got the elevators pretty much under control within three or four hundred feet. |

| 3:43:13 | Airport Tower: | United 232 heavy; roger. Understand you do have elevators under control. |

| 3:43:18 | Aircraft: (Captain) | Negative. We don't have it. We are better. That's all. |

| 3:45:09 | Airport Tower: | United 232 there is a small airport at twelve o'clock and seven miles. The runway is four thousand feet long. |

| 3:45:20 | Aircraft: (First Officer) | I'm controlling it myself right now. As soon as the |

captain gets back on he'll give me a hand here. He's talking on the PA right now to the passengers.

3:46:03   Aircraft:
(Captain)

We're starting a turn back to the airport . . . ah . . . we have . . . since we have no hydraulics, breaking is gonna really be a problem. Would suggest the equipment be toward the far end of the runway and, ah, I think under the circumstances, regardless of the condition of the airplane when we stop, we're going to evacuate. So you might notify the ground crew pretty much that we're going to do that.

3:46:30   Airport
Tower:

United 232 heavy. Sir, if you can continue that left turn to about a, ah, two twenty heading sir, that'll take you to the airport.

3:46:40   Aircraft:
(Captain)

OK, let's, ah, start this sucker down a little bit. Anybody got any ideas?

3:46:43   Aircraft:
(Captain)

How do we get the gear down?

3:46:45	Aircraft: (Training Pilot)	Well, they can free fall. The only thing is we alternate gear . . . we got the doors down.
3:46:48	Aircraft: (First Officer)	We're gonna have trouble stopping too.
3:46:50	Aircraft: (Captain)	Oh yeah, we don't have any brakes. . . well, we have some brakes.
3:46:53	Aircraft: (First Officer)	Accumulator is . . . ah . . . just one shot.
3:46:59	Aircraft: (Training Pilot)	One shot deal. Just mash it. Mash it once. That's all you get.
3:47:05	Aircraft: (Second Officer)	All we got in both sides?
3:47:08	Aircraft: (Training Pilot)	Yeah.
3:50:12	Aircraft: (Captain)	Well mamma, we'll miss those baseball games after all.
3:51:12	Airport Tower:	United 232 heavy; you're going to have to widen out just slightly to your left sir . . . ah . . . to make the turn to final and also it'll take you away from the city.

| 3:51:21 | Aircraft: (Captain) | Whatever you do keep us away from the city. |

| 3:52:34 | Airport Tower: | United 232 heavy; how steep a right turn can you make? |

| 3:52:37 | Aircraft: (Captain) | About a thirty degree bank. |

| 3:52:59 | Airport Tower: | United 232 heavy; be advised there is a four lane highway up in that area, sir, if you can pick that up. |

| 3:53:06 | Aircraft: (Captain) | OK, we'll see what we can do here. We've already put the gear down and . . . ah . . . we're going to have to be putting on something solid if we can. |

| 3:54:40 | Airport Tower: | United 232 heavy; roger. Can you pick up a road or something up there? |

| 3:54:43 | Aircraft: (First Officer) | We're trying it. |

| 3:55:20 | Airport Tower: | United 232 heavy; the airport is . . . ah . . . about . . . eighteen miles southeast of your |

		position, about two twenty on the heading, but we're going to need you southbound away from the city first if you can hold one eighty heading.
3:55:31	Aircraft: (First Officer)	We're trying, trying to get it to the right now.
3:55:39	Airport Tower:	United 232 heavy; advise if you can pick up a road or anything where you can possibly land it.
3:55:44	Aircraft: (First Officer)	OK, we're . . . ah . . . we're hundred eighty degree heading now. What do you want?
3:55:47	Airport Tower:	United 232; if you can hold the altitude, the one eighty heading will work fine for about, oh, seven miles.
3:55:51	Aircraft: (Captain)	OK, we're trying to turn back.
3:56:25	Airport Tower:	United 232 heavy, can you hold that heading sir?
3:56:27	Aircraft: (First Officer)	Yeah, we're on it now for a little while.

3:56:29	Airport Tower:	United 232; roger. That heading will put you, oh, currently, fifteen miles northeast of the airport. If you can hold that, it'll put you on about a three mile final.

3:56:36   Aircraft: (First Officer)

OK, we'll give it heck.

3:57:30   Aircraft: (Captain)

We're starting down a little bit now. We got a little better control of the elevator. It's not full, but a little.

3:57:39   Airport Tower:

United 232 heavy; roger. The airport is currently at your one o'clock position, one zero mouse.

United 232 heavy; if you can't make the airport, sir, there is an interstate that runs, ah, north to south at the east side of the airport . . . ah . . . a four lane interstate.

3:58:07   Aircraft: (Captain)

We're just passing it right now. We're gonna try for the airport. We have the runway in sight. We'll be with you shortly. Thanks a lot for your help.

3:58:24	Airport Tower:	United 232 heavy; winds currently three six zero at one three sixty at eleven. You're cleared to land on any runway.
3:58:31	Aircraft: (Captain)	(laughter) Roger. (laughter) You want to be particular and make it a runway huh?
3:58:38	Aircraft: (Captain)	Let's hear the wind one more time.
3:58:41	Airport Tower:	Zero one; zero at one one.
3:58:47	Aircraft: (Captain)	We were all talking at once. Let's hear it one more time.
3:58:50	Airport Tower:	Zero one; zero at one one and there is a runway . . . ah . . . that's closed, sir, that could probably work too. It runs northeast to southwest.
3:58:59	Aircraft: (Captain)	We're pretty well lined up on this one here, or think we will be.
3:59:08	Airport Tower:	United 232 heavy; ah . . . roger, sir. Yeah, that's a closed runway. That'll work, sir. We're getting the equipment off the

		runway and they'll line up for that one.
3:59:14	Aircraft: Captain)	How long is it?
3:59:22	Airport Tower:	Sixty six hundred feet. Six thousand six hundred. And the equipment is coming off.
3:59:34	Airport Tower:	Ah, at the end of the runway, it's just a wide open field so, sir, so the length won't be a problem.
4:00:09	Aircraft: (First Officer)	Left, left, left, left, left, left, left, left, left, left.
4:00:16	Aircraft	(sound of impact)

**YOUR COMMENTS ABOUT THIS BOOK
ARE WELCOME!**

Please send correspondence to:

Jerry Schemmel
Victory Publishing
P.O. Box 621129
Littleton, CO 80162

BOOK ORDER FORM

TELEPHONE ORDERS: Toll Free: 888-246-7362

FAX ORDERS: 303-904-0397

MAIL ORDERS: Victory Publishing
P.O. Box 621129
Littleton, CO 80162

*P*lease send me _____ copies of *Chosen to Live*

@ $22.95 per book _____

Colorado residents add $1.65 per book sales tax _____

Shipping: $2.00 for the first book;
$1.00 for each additional book _____

TOTAL ORDER _____

Payment: ☐ Check
☐ *Please charge my:* ☐ **VISA** ☐ **MasterCard** ☐ **AMERICAN EXPRESS**
Card Number _____

Expiration Date: Month_____ Year _____

Name on card _____

Signature _____

Ship To:

Name _____

Address _____

City / State / Zip _____

Telephone (   ) _____

Mail checks made payable to :
Victory Publishing • P.O. Box 621129 • Littleton, CO 80162
(Please allow 2 to 4 weeks for delivery)